Jose Mou
Attacking Sessions

114 Practices from Goal Analysis of Real Madrid's 4-2-3-1

WRITTEN BY MICHAIL TSOKAKTSIDIS

PUBLISHED BY

Jose Mourinho
Attacking Sessions

114 Practices from Goal Analysis of Real Madrid's 4-2-3-1

First Published April 2013 by SoccerTutor.com

Info@soccertutor.com | www.SoccerTutor.com

UK: 0208 1234 007 | **US:** (305) 767 4443 | **ROTW:** +44 208 1234 007
ISBN: 978-0-9566752-9-3

Author
Michail Tsokaktsidis © 2013

Edited by
Alex Fitzgerald - SoccerTutor.com

Cover Design by
Alex Macrides, Think Out Of The Box Ltd.
Email: design@thinkootb.com Tel: +44 (0) 208 144 3550

Diagrams
Diagram designs by SoccerTutor.com. All the diagrams in this book have been created using SoccerTutor.com Tactics Manager Software available from **www.SoccerTutor.com**

Note: While every effort has been made to ensure the technical accuracy of the content of this book, neither the author nor publishers can accept any responsibility for any injury or loss sustained as a result of the use of this material.

MEET THE AUTHOR

MICHAIL TSOKAKTSIDIS

m.tsokaktsidis@gmail.com

- UEFA A Coaching licence
- Bachelor Degree in Physical Education, specialising in Soccer Conditioning.

I am 38 years old and started playing football at the age of 10 for F.C Doxa Dramas in Greece. I played in all the age levels before progressing to the first team when I was 19 years old. I played for 10 years as a professional at all levels of Greek football for the following teams: Doxa Dramas, Iltex Likoi (WOLVES), Agrotikos Asteras, Ethnikos K., Pandramaikos and Olimpiakos Volou.

During my career I won 6 championships with 5 different teams. At the age of 29 I stopped playing and completed my studies in fitness conditioning and football coaching. I was also a student of the UEFA coaching schools (H.F.F in Greece) and I am a fully certified UEFA A' licence coach.

I started my coaching career in youth football for 3 years and for the last 4 years I have been a head coach in 3 different semiprofessional teams in Greece (winning 2 championships). The aim is to develop young players to be professional footballers. My desire is to work at a higher level elsewhere in Europe.

Football is my main focus in life and I have a deep passion for coaching. From very early I was interested in studying training methods as well as to observe and analyse how they are successfully applied (in all phases of the game). I love to learn from the great and successful teams who help to evolve the game.

For my first book I wanted to use my skills to create great content for coaches all over the world to improve their training sessions. I decided to analyse a team coached by one of the most successful coaches in the last 10 years, Jose Mourinho. The season in which all these goals were scored was 2011-2012 when Jose lead Real Madrid to the Spanish championship (La Liga).

I think this is a book which provides content that has not been produced before. We have combined a comprehensive analysis of the phases of play which lead to goals with training exercises that can be used for coaches to train the 4-2-3-1.

1. We analyse Jose Mourinho's tactics and the phases of play which lead to Real Madrid's best goals and how to recognise and find solutions against different opposition's formations and tactical situations.

2. We created specific practices to train how to apply the same objectives to your team and achieve the same results.

In life, I believe it is not what you own that matters, but what you create. So I have decided to make this book. My favourite motto is 'You can always do much more.'

COACHING FORMAT

1. Goal Analysis.

2. Full Training Session from the Goal Analysis.

- Technical / Functional unopposed practices
- Tactical opposed practices
- Progressions and variations

KEY

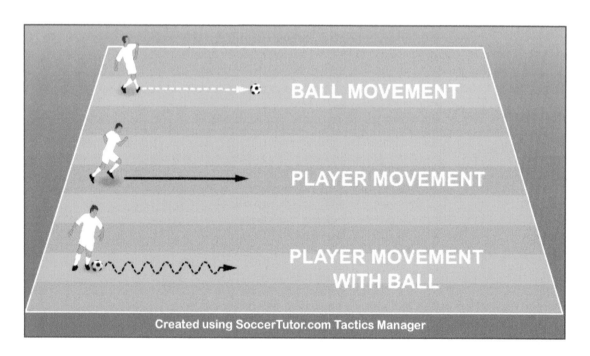

BALL MOVEMENT

PLAYER MOVEMENT

PLAYER MOVEMENT WITH BALL

Created using SoccerTutor.com Tactics Manager

CONTENTS

Real Madrid Statistics During the 2011-2012 Season 11
Outline Of Jose Mourinho's Attacking Tactics...12
Real Madrid's Players 13

CHAPTER 1
Attacking against Opponents who use a Deep Defensive Line 14

Goal Analysis: One-Two Combination and Quick Final Ball 18
SESSION FOR THIS TOPIC (7 Practices)
1. Passing and One-Two Combination Play 19
2. Quick One-Two Combination Play..20
3. One-Two Combination and Final Ball...21
4. One-Two Combination and Final Ball with 2 Options 22
5. Double One-Two Combination and Final Ball 23
6. One-Two Combination Play with Final Ball in a SSG 24
7. Inside Supporting Runs in a 4 Zone Game 25

Goal Analysis: One Touch Combination Play with a 3rd Man Run.......................................27
SESSION FOR THIS TOPIC (5 Practices)
1. Short and Long Passing Combination Play 29
2. Quick Passing Combination, 3rd Man Run and Finish..30
3. Quick Combination, 3rd Man Run, Final Ball and Finish 31
4. Through Balls & 3rd Man Runs in a Small Sided Game 32
5. Quick Combinations & 3rd Man Runs in a 4 Zone Game 34

Goal Analysis: 3rd Man Overlapping Run & Final Ball Behind Defensive Line 36
SESSION FOR THIS TOPIC (7 Practices)
1. Dribble inside to Create Space for 3rd Man Overlap 38
2. Dribble Inside with 3rd Man Overlap and Finish..39
3. Combination, 3rd Man Overlap and Final Ball 40
4. Dribble Inside, 3rd Man Overlap and Final Ball 41
5. Dribble Inside, 3rd Man Overlap, Support and Final Pass..42
6. 3rd Man Overlapping Runs with Side Zones in a SSG (1) 43
7. 3rd Man Overlapping Runs with Side Zones in a SSG (2)...44

Goal Analysis: 1v1 on the Flank with Runs from the Centre into the Box 45
SESSION FOR THIS TOPIC *(6 Practices)*
1. Timing of Runs with Short Crossing and Finishing...48
2. Switching Play and Crossing in a Position Specific Practice...50
3. 1v1 on the Flanks: Crossing & Finishing with Side Zones..51
4. 1v1 in the Centre and on the Flanks with Side Zones 52
5. 2v2 on the Flanks - Crossing & Finishing with Side Zones 53
6. 2v2 on the Flanks - Switching Play, Crossing & Finishing..54

Goal Analysis: Intelligent Positioning in the Box with Quick Finishing 55
SESSION FOR THIS TOPIC *(3 Practices)*
1. Quick Finishing in and Around the Penalty Area 56
2. Transition Play - Winning the 2nd Ball with Quick Finishing 57
3. Winning the Ball Back Immediately in a Dynamic Game 58

Goal Analysis: Full Back's In Advanced Positions: Crossing and Finishing...59
SESSION FOR THIS TOPIC *(2 Practices)*
1. Crossing and Finishing with Advanced Full Backs (1)..60
2. Crossing and Finishing with Advanced Full Backs (2)..61

Goal Analysis: Switching Play to Change the Point of Attack 62
SESSION FOR THIS TOPIC *(4 Practices)*
1. Utilising Width and Switching Play in a Small Sided Game...67
2. Switching Play with Advanced Full Backs in a SSG (1)..68
3. Switching Play with Advanced Full Backs in a SSG (2)..69
4. Using Width and Creating Space in and Around the Box...70

Goal Analysis: Timed Runs in Between the Full Back and Centre Back...71
SESSION FOR THIS TOPIC *(3 Practices)*
1. Passing in Behind the Defensive Line in a 9 Zone SSG..73
2. Exploiting Space in Behind with Diagonal Runs in a SSG 74
3. Timing Runs in Between Defenders Who Use a Deep Line..75

Goal Analysis: Attacking in Behind the Defensive Line Through the Centre...76
SESSION FOR THIS TOPIC *(4 Practices)*
1. 6v6 (+2) Passing into the 'Goal Zone' Small Sided Game..77
2. 6v6 (+2) Support Play in a 1v1 Zonal Dynamic Game 78
3. 7v7 (+2) Runs in Behind and Finishing in a SSG 79
4. Receiving in Behind the Defensive Line - 9v9 80

Goal Analysis: Timing Runs in Behind to be Onside 81
SESSION FOR THIS TOPIC *(4 Practices)*
1. Attacking Combinations & Finishing with the Offside Rule 82

2. 6v5 (+GK) Attacking and Finishing with the Offside Rule (1)..83
3. 6v5 (+GK) Attacking and Finishing with the Offside Rule (2)..84
4. Attacking and Finishing with the Offside Rule in a SSG 85

CHAPTER 2
Attacking against Opponents who use a Middle Defensive Line 86

Goal Analysis: Creating Space for 1v1 Situations on the Flank 88
SESSION FOR THIS TOPIC *(5 Practices)*
1. Creating Space on the Flank and Timing Runs from the Centre in an Unopposed Practice 91
2. Creating Space on the Flank and Timing Runs from the Centre in an Opposed Practice 92
3. 2v2 on the Flanks with Crossing and Finishing...93
4. 2v2 on the Flanks with Support from the Centre..93
5. Creating a 1v1 Situation on the Flank 94

Goal Analysis: Midfield Forward Runs in Behind the Defence 95
SESSION FOR THIS TOPIC *(4 Practices)*
1. Forward Runs and Through Balls in a Zonal Game...98
2. Timing Runs in Between Defenders in a 4 Zone Game...99
3. Timing Runs in Between Defenders in a 9v9 Game...100
4. Timing Runs in a Position Specific Zonal Practice...101

Goal Analysis: Through Balls from the Flank into the Centre & in Behind 102
SESSION FOR THIS TOPIC *(4 Practices)*
1. 6v6 (+2) 'End Zone' Final Ball Game...105
2. Diagonal Through Balls from Wide Areas (1) 106
3. Diagonal Through Balls from Wide Areas (2) 107
4. Passing in Behind a Middle Defensive Line in a 9v9 Game...107

Goal Analysis: Long Switch of Play to Create Space for a Final Ball......................................108
PRACTICE FOR THIS TOPIC
1. Switching Play and Through Balls Against a Middle Defensive Line in a 5 Zone Position Specific Practice........109

CHAPTER 3
Attacking against Opponents who use a High Defensive Line 110

Goal Analysis: Playing the Ball in Behind a High Defensive Line 112
SESSION FOR THIS TOPIC *(4 Practices)*
1. 4 Zone Possession Game...114
2. Position Specific 7v7 (+1) Possession Game 115
3. Building Up Play Through the Lines in a Position Specific Practice..117
4. Playing in Behind a High Defensive Line in an 11v11 Game..119

Goal Analysis: Building Up Play against Opponent's who Press High 120
SESSION FOR THIS TOPIC (5 Practices)
1. Breaking Through Pressure Possession Game..121
2. Dynamic Transitional Possession Game in the 4-2-3-1..122
3. Playing Through the Lines in a 3 Zone Small Sided Game..123
4. Breaking Through Pressure High Up the Pitch in a 3 Zone Game (1)...............................124
5. Breaking Through Pressure High Up the Pitch in a 3 Zone Game (2)...............................125

CHAPTER 4
The Transition from Defence to Attack in the Low Zone...................................... 126

Goal Analysis: Creating and Taking Advantage of 1v1 / 2v2 Situations 130
SESSION FOR THIS TOPIC (2 Practices)
1. Unopposed Fast Break Attack Practice 132
2. Opposed Fast Break Attack with 1v1 / 2v2 Situations 133

Goal Analysis: Quick Counter Attacking from the Low Zone..134
SESSION FOR THIS TOPIC (3 Practices)
1. Transition & Support Play in a 3 Zone Dynamic Game..135
2. Transition & Support Play with Side Players...137
3. 11v11 Transition & Support Play in a 4 Zone Game 137

Goal Analysis: Exploiting the Weak Side of the Opposition 138
SESSION FOR THIS TOPIC (5 Practices)
1. 3 Team Counter Attacking Small Sided Game..140
2. Dynamic 3 Team Counter Attacking Small Sided Game..141
3. Playing Wide and Switching Play in a Transition Game 142
4. Exploiting the Weak Side of the Opponent in a 3 Zone Transition Game 143
5. Exploiting the Weak Side of the Opponent in a 3 Zone Transition Game using a Full Pitch ...144

Goal Analysis: Long Pass to Switch Play to the Weak Side on the Break 145
SESSION FOR THIS TOPIC (2 Practices)
1. Fast Break and Switch of Play in a 5 Zone Game (1)...147
2. Fast Break and Switch of Play in a 5 Zone Game (2)...148

Goal Analysis: Creating and Exploiting Space on the Flanks 149
SESSION FOR THIS TOPIC (5 Practices)
1. Defensive Organisation to Win Possession with Quick Break from the Low Zone................151
2. Fast Combinations, Support and Finishing Practice 152
3. Fast Combinations, Support and Finishing Transition Game..153
4. Counter Attacking with a 4v3 Situation in a 3 Zone Game 154
5. Counter Attacking with a 4v4 Situation in a 3 Zone Game 155

Goal Analysis: Breaking from the Low Zone:
Causing Imbalance in a Defensive Line with a Delayed Pass 156
SESSION FOR THIS TOPIC *(2 Practices)*
1. Support Play in a Low Zone Transition Small Sided Game 158
2. Fast Break Attacks in Behind the Defensive Line in a Low Zone Transition Game 159

CHAPTER 5
The Transition from Defence to Attack in the Middle Zone 160

Goal Analysis: Breaking from the Middle Zone:
Causing Imbalance in a Defensive Line with a Delayed Pass 162
SESSION FOR THIS TOPIC *(3 Practices)*
1. Win the Ball, Dribble, Delayed Final Ball and Finish..164
2. Win the Ball, Dribble and Delayed Pass in an Opposed Practice 165
3. Win the Ball, Dribble and Delayed Pass against a High Line 166

Goal Analysis: Winning Possession in the Centre: Breaking vs a High Line 167
SESSION FOR THIS TOPIC *(3 Practices)*
1. Interceptions and Fast Counter Attacking in a 3 Zone Game.....................................171
2. Fast Counter Attacking from the Middle Zone (1) 172
3. Fast Counter Attacking from the Middle Zone (2) 173

Goal Analysis: Overload Fast Break Attack...174
SESSION FOR THIS TOPIC *(3 Practices)*
1. 2v2 / 3v2 Defence to Attack Transition Duel Game..175
2. Fast Break Attacks in a 2 Zone Support Play Game 177
3. 3v2 Support Play in an Attacking / Defending Duel Game 178

CHAPTER 6
The Transition from Defence to Attack in the High Zone 179

Goal Analysis: Transition from Attack to Defence & then Defence to Attack 181
SESSION FOR THIS TOPIC *(4 Practices)*
1. Passing, Pressing and Fast Break in an Unopposed Practice......................................184
2. Possession, Winning the Ball and Counter Attacking in a Dynamic Game (1)............186
3. Counter Attacking in a Dynamic Game (2) 188
4. Counter Attacking in a Dynamic Game (3) 188

CHAPTER 7
Building Up Play from the Low Zone To The High Zone.. 189

Goal Analysis: Passing Through the Midfield Line from the Back 191
SESSION FOR THIS TOPIC (5 Practices)
1. Possession & Forward Passing in a 3 Zone Dynamic Game...193
2. 6v6 (+2) Possession & Forward Passing in a 3 Zone Dynamic Game 194
3. Passing Through the Midfield Line Transition Game 195
4. Passing Through the Midfield Line in a 3 Team Dynamic Transition Game...........................196
5. Passing Through Midfield Line & Finishing in a 5 Zone Game 197

Goal Analysis: Building Up Play from the Back Through the Centre 198
SESSION FOR THIS TOPIC (2 Practices)
1. 9v9 (+2) Position Specific 5 Zone Possession Game 201
2. Building Up Play from the Back in 1v1 / 2v2 / 3v3 Zones...203

Goal Analysis: Build Up Play with a 4v4 Situation on the Flank 204
PRACTICE FOR THIS TOPIC
1. Building Up Play From the Back with a 4v4 Central Zone 205

Goal Analysis: Creating 1v1 and 2v1 Situations Near the Penalty Area 206
SESSION FOR THIS TOPIC (3 Practices)
1. 'End to End' 3v3 (+3) Possession Game...207
2. 'End to End' 5v5 (+1) Possession Game...208
3. Build Up Through the Centre and Support Play in a 9 Zone Dynamic 10v10 Game.............209

REAL MADRID STATISTICS DURING THE 2011-2012 SEASON

In the 2011-2012 season Real Madrid were best attacking team in La Liga, scoring 7 more goals than Barcelona and finishing 9 points clear at the top.

Pos	Team	Pld	W	D	L	GF	GA	GD	Pts
1	Real Madrid (C)	38	32	4	2	121	32	89	100
2	Barcelona	38	28	7	3	114	29	85	91

Real averaged **3.18** goals per game.

They scored in 35 of their 38 games in La Liga.

The most goals in a single match was against Osasuna on 6th Nov 2011.

 7 - 1

 But how did Real Madrid attack so well and score so many goals?

And what training drills can we create to practice these same situations?

OUTLINE OF JOSE MOURINHO'S ATTACKING TACTICS

How do Real Madrid recognise situations and find solutions to tactical problems against different opponents?

We analyse Mourinho's tactics against different teams:

- Who defend deep
- Who defend with a middle line
- Who defend with a high line

Also how did Real Madrid score so many goals in the transition from defence to attack? We analyse:

- Winning the ball and counter attacking from the low zone
- Winning the ball and counter attacking from the middle zone
- Winning the ball and counter attacking from the high zone

In the positive transition phase of the game Real Madrid were exceptional and are described as 'the best counter attacking team in the world.'

REAL MADRID'S PLAYERS

2011-2012 SEASON (4-2-3-1 FORMATION)

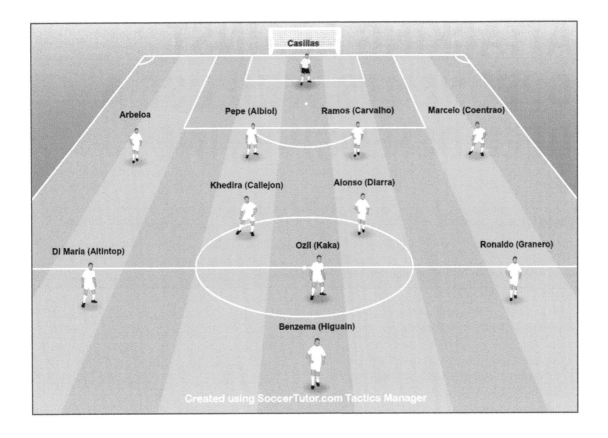

CHAPTER 1

ATTACKING AGAINST OPPONENTS WHO USE A DEEP DEFENSIVE LINE

CHAPTER 1
Attacking against Opponents who use a Deep Defensive Line 14

Goal Analysis: One-Two Combination and Quick Final Ball 18
SESSION FOR THIS TOPIC *(7 Practices)*
1. Passing and One-Two Combination Play 19
2. Quick One-Two Combination Play.. 20
3. One-Two Combination and Final Ball 21
4. One-Two Combination and Final Ball with 2 Options 22
5. Double One-Two Combination and Final Ball 23
6. One-Two Combination Play with Final Ball in a SSG 24
7. Inside Supporting Runs in a 4 Zone Game 25

Goal Analysis: One Touch Combination Play with a 3rd Man Run 27
SESSION FOR THIS TOPIC *(5 Practices)*
1. Short and Long Passing Combination Play 29
2. Quick Passing Combination, 3rd Man Run and Finish... 30
3. Quick Combination, 3rd Man Run, Final Ball and Finish 31
4. Through Balls & 3rd Man Runs in a Small Sided Game 32
5. Quick Combinations & 3rd Man Runs in a 4 Zone Game 34

Goal Analysis: 3rd Man Overlapping Run & Final Ball Behind Defensive Line 36
SESSION FOR THIS TOPIC *(7 Practices)*
1. Dribble inside to Create Space for 3rd Man Overlap 38
2. Dribble Inside with 3rd Man Overlap and Finish... 39
3. Combination, 3rd Man Overlap and Final Ball 40

4. Dribble Inside, 3rd Man Overlap and Final Ball..41
5. Dribble Inside, 3rd Man Overlap, Support and Final Pass...42
6. 3rd Man Overlapping Runs with Side Zones in a SSG (1)...43
7. 3rd Man Overlapping Runs with Side Zones in a SSG (2)...44

Goal Analysis: 1v1 on the Flank with Runs from the Centre into the Box 45
SESSION FOR THIS TOPIC *(6 Practices)*
1. Timing of Runs with Short Crossing and Finishing...48
2. Switching Play and Crossing in a Position Specific Practice..50
3. 1v1 on the Flanks: Crossing & Finishing with Side Zones..51
4. 1v1 in the Centre and on the Flanks with Side Zones...52
5. 2v2 on the Flanks - Crossing & Finishing with Side Zones..53
6. 2v2 on the Flanks - Switching Play, Crossing & Finishing...54

Goal Analysis: Intelligent Positioning in the Box with Quick Finishing 55
SESSION FOR THIS TOPIC *(3 Practices)*
1. Quick Finishing in and Around the Penalty Area 56
2. Transition Play - Winning the 2nd Ball with Quick Finishing...57
3. Winning the Ball Back Immediately in a Dynamic Game 58

Goal Analysis: Full Back's In Advanced Positions: Crossing and Finishing 59
SESSION FOR THIS TOPIC *(2 Practices)*
1. Crossing and Finishing with Advanced Full Backs (1)..60
2. Crossing and Finishing with Advanced Full Backs (2)..61

Goal Analysis: Switching Play to Change the Point of Attack 62
SESSION FOR THIS TOPIC *(4 Practices)*
1. Utilising Width and Switching Play in a Small Sided Game...67
2. Switching Play with Advanced Full Backs in a SSG (1)..68
3. Switching Play with Advanced Full Backs in a SSG (2)..69
4. Using Width and Creating Space in and Around the Box..70

Goal Analysis: Timed Runs in Between the Full Back and Centre Back 71
SESSION FOR THIS TOPIC *(3 Practices)*
1. Passing in Behind the Defensive Line in a 9 Zone SSG..73
2. Exploiting Space in Behind with Diagonal Runs in a SSG 74
3. Timing Runs in Between Defenders Who Use a Deep Line..75

Goal Analysis: Attacking in Behind the Defensive Line Through the Centre...............................76
SESSION FOR THIS TOPIC *(4 Practices)*
1. 6v6 (+2) Passing into the 'Goal Zone' Small Sided Game..77
2. 6v6 (+2) Support Play in a 1v1 Zonal Dynamic Game...78
3. 7v7 (+2) Runs in Behind and Finishing in a SSG 79
4. Receiving in Behind the Defensive Line - 9v9 80

Goal Analysis: Timing Runs in Behind to be Onside 81

SESSION FOR THIS TOPIC *(4 Practices)*

1. Attacking Combinations & Finishing with the Offside Rule 82
2. 6v5 (+GK) Attacking and Finishing with the Offside Rule (1)... 83
3. 6v5 (+GK) Attacking and Finishing with the Offside Rule (2)... 84
4. Attacking and Finishing with the Offside Rule in a SSG 85

ATTACKING AGAINST OPPONENTS WHO USE A DEEP DEFENSIVE LINE

Real Madrid played against many teams who defended using a deep line in the 2011-2012 season. In these matches Jose Mourinho and his players had to find solutions against teams who had many players (minimum 8) behind the ball. They needed to break down these defences who were very organised and create opportunities to score goals. There are 2 main elements to this, the first was to exploit their own attacking strengths (individual and tactical team elements) and secondly to exploit the weaknesses of the opponent. We have outlined 6 conclusion of Real Madrid's tactics in these situations:

1. When facing opponents who have many players behind the ball and who do not play active defence, mainly focusing on the space rather than the player with the ball, Real Madrid attacked using quick combination play. The use of combinations between 3 players was especially noticeable (capitalising on 3rd man runs).

2. Against opponents who were defensively weak on the flanks, Real Madrid tried to exploit 1v1 situations, especially on the left with Ronaldo. The other players would leave the space for the left forward (Ronaldo) or the right forward (Di Maria) and use well timed runs to take up good positions in the penalty area

3. Against opponents who squeezed the play and closed down well around the penalty area in numbers, Real would use their full backs high up on the flanks and a minimum of 4 players would enter the box. The 2 central midfield players would be positioned just outside of the box to provide balance and to be ready to win the second ball or be the first defender for a possible counter attack.

4. When the opposition was very well organised and played with ball oriented defence, the objective of Real Madrid was to maintain possession and make quick switches of play. They used the full width of the pitch very well, moving the ball from the strong side of the opponent to the weak side quickly and efficiently to change the direction of play.

5. Jose Mourinho's team looked to use a numerical advantage (2v1) at the side of the pitch when a team had many players in the centre (which would leave the full backs uncovered). So when passes were played to the flanks, one player from the centre of the pitch (midfielder or forward) would make a diagonal cutting run in behind the opponent's full back and in between the full back and central defender.

6. Lastly, we have the solutions when attacking through the centre, especially when the opponents did not close down/press the player in possession. Real would use their good dribbling ability to run at the defenders in central areas and would take opportunities to play the final ball or beat the defensive line when the opposition had slower central defenders.

GOAL ANALYSIS
One-Two Combination and Quick Final Ball

14-Jan-12
Mallorca 1-2 Real Madrid (1st Goal): Higuain - Assist: Ozil

Ozil cuts inside from the left flank and plays a 1-2 with Benzema. This moment is very difficult for the opponent to track and a defensive imbalance is created.

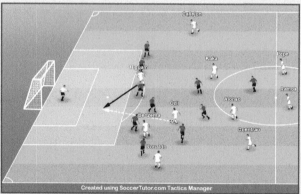

One defender moves to close down Ozil. With perfect timing, Higuain makes a run into the space in behind the defensive line. And Ozil also shows great timing with his pass into the space for Higuain.

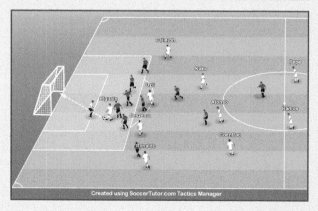

Higuain uses one touch to score past the goalkeeper

SESSION FOR THIS TOPIC *(7 Practices)*

1. Passing and One-Two Combination Play

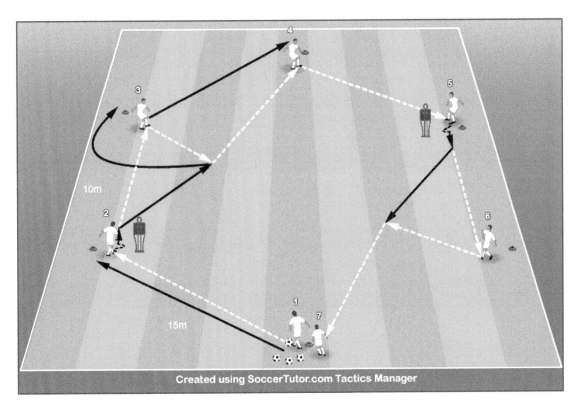

Created using SoccerTutor.com Tactics Manager

Objective

To develop one-two combinations and accurate passing in team play.

Description

In an area 30 yards x 30 yards, we use 7 players, 6 cones and 2 mannequins.

Player 1 passes to Player 2 and moves into Player 2's starting position. Player 2 passes to Player 3 and moves inside to receive a pass back and passes to Player 4 (Player 3 moves into Player 4's starting position). The sequence is repeated as shown on the other side when Player 4 makes his first pass. When the final pass is played to Player 7 he becomes Player 1 and the full sequence starts again.

Coaching Points

1. The emphasis is on a good directional first touch from Player's 2 and 5 with with the second touch being a pass.

2. The correct body shape should be monitored (opening up) and receiving/passing with the back foot (foot furthest away from the ball).

3. Use the part of the foot suitable for the distances in each part of the drill and the players must anticipate the next movement to make it flow.

4. Accuracy of pass, weight of pass and good communication are all key elements for this practice.

VARIATION

2. Quick One-Two Combination Play

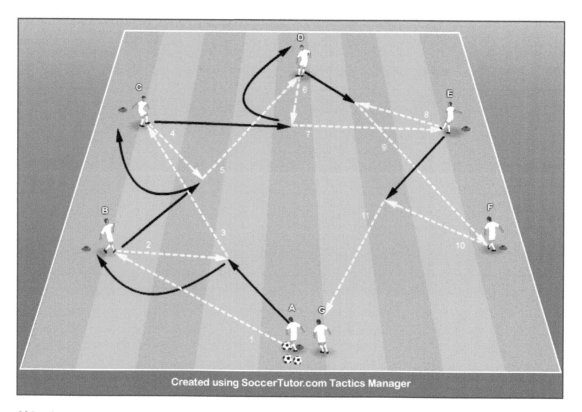

Created using SoccerTutor.com Tactics Manager

Objective

To develop one-two combinations and accurate passing in team play.

Description

We have removed the mannequins for this variation.

We start with 1 ball as player A passes to player B. Player B passes back to Player A who runs onto the ball and passes to Player C. Player C passes to Player B who runs onto the ball and passes to Player D. The sequence continues as shown in the diagram by the numbered order of the passes. The final pass is made by Player E to Player G who starts the sequence again.

All players run to the next position after making their second pass (A to B, B to C etc.) The players should use 1 touch. Put an extra man at Position D to play with 2 balls starting from Positions A and D at the same time.

Coaching Points

1. The accuracy and weight of the pass needs to be correct.
2. The rhythm and timing of the movement together with the pass is key.
3. Make sure the players communicate with their teammates and heads are up.

PROGRESSION

3. One-Two Combination and Final Ball

Created using SoccerTutor.com Tactics Manager

Description

Now we have a functional practice, with 2 central defenders or central midfielders, 2 full backs, 2 wide forwards and 1 striker.

The ball starts with the central defender or midfielder (4) who passes wide to the full back (3). The left back dribbles forward and passes to the left winger/forward (11), then runs inside to collect a pass back from 11. No.3 receives the ball and drives inside and plays a well timed pass into the space behind the defensive line for the striker (9). The striker first runs horizontally and then diagonally to curve his run and prevent being offside. He then receives in space and shoots at goal.

Coaching Points

1. The accuracy and weight of the pass needs to be correct.

2. The timing of the movement for checking away (from marker) and moving to meet the ball is very important so that quick play is maintained.

3. Player 3 needs to make a directional first touch forward through the cones and should dribble inside at speed.

VARIATION

4. One-Two Combination and Final Ball with 2 Options

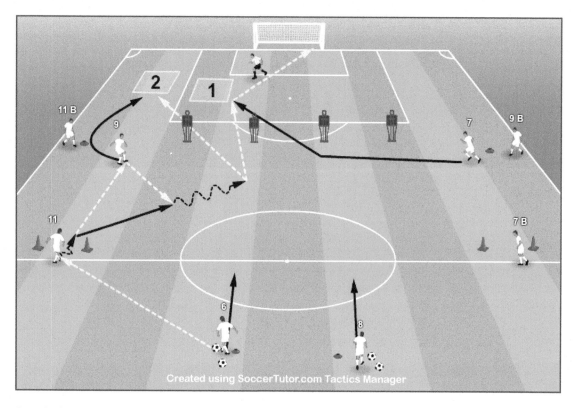

Description

Here we use the same starting positions but in the centre of the pitch we have 2 central midfielders and on the side we have an attacking combination play between the wide forward and the striker (not the full back).

The wide forward (11) plays the same 1-2 combination as the full back in the previous example, but this time there are 2 passing options in behind the defensive line (7 or 9). The first option (Pass to 7) leads directly to a shot on goal.

In the second option the striker (9) is in a good position to cross; 7 can run to the near post and 11 to the far post with the central midfielders (6 and 8) approaching the penalty area.

We play the drill from both sides. From the right, 8 plays to 7b, who plays a 1-2 with 9b and dribbles inside. 7b has 2 options; 9b out wide or 11b who makes a run in between the central defenders.

Coaching Points

1. The runs in behind the defensive line need to be sharp and curved/angled at the right point to practice beating offside and timed correctly to meet the pass.

VARIATION

5. Double One-Two Combination and Final Ball

Description

In this variation, the wide forward (11) plays the ball back to the central midfielder (6) who plays the ball into the striker. The wide forward makes the same run inside again to receive the ball, but this time plays a first time ball in behind the defensive line.

He has 2 options: 1. Pass to the striker on the left flank.

2. Pass in between the opposition full back and central defender for No.7 to shoot on goal.

PROGRESSION

6. One-Two Combination Play with Final Ball in a SSG

Created using SoccerTutor.com Tactics Manager

Objective

To develop one-two combinations and playing the final ball in behind the defensive line.

Description 7 v 7 (+ 3 Neutral Players)

In an area of 70 yards x 55 yards we divide the pitch into 3 zones. The central zone is 32 yards x 55 yards and the 2 'Final Zones' are 16 yards x 52 yards. Both teams have 6 players each inside the central zone in a 2-3-1 formation. There are 3 neutrals playing with the team in possession (1 in the central zone & 1 in each 'Final Zone').

There should be good cooperation in attack with the neutral players. A 1-2 with a 3rd man combination has to be played with a neutral player in the 'Final Zone' before a final ball can be played to a teammate into this zone who then shoots on goal.

Rule Options

1. There are no defenders allowed in the 'Final Zones' but limited touches should be applied.

2. In the final zone, the defenders are allowed but they must be passive.

3. In the final zone, there must be 1 less defender than attacker. The attackers have limited touches.

4. In the final zone, the defenders are fully active and there are unlimited touches.

Coaching Points

1. Encourage one-twos with 3rd man combinations to break down the pressure and move up the pitch more quickly.

2. The attacking player in the final zone should get his shot off quickly and focus on accuracy.

PROGRESSION

7. Inside Supporting Runs in a 4 Zone Game

Objective

To develop one-two combinations and playing the final ball in behind the defensive line.

Description 9 v 9

Using half a full size pitch, divide into 4 zones as shown in the diagram. We put 3 goals on the halfway line; 1 full size goal in the centre and 1 mini goal either side. The white team are defending the end with 3 goals and the red team defend the end with 1 goal.

Both teams have 8 players. The white team is using a 2-2-3-1 (or 4-3-1) formation (with 2 full backs, 2 central midfielders, 2 wide forwards, 1 attacking midfielder and 1 striker). The other team (red) are in a 4-4 formation.

In the side zones, only the wide players are allowed (numbers 2,3,7 & 11 of both teams). The white team has possession and must have good cooperation and use 1-2 combinations with 3rd man runs to create goal scoring opportunities in the final zone (in behind the red defence).

The other team defends the final zone and can counter attack, scoring in any of the 3 goals on the halfway line.

When the ball goes out, the game always begins again with the white team's goalkeeper.

Rule Options (Including Progressions)

1. 2,3,7 & 11 of the red team are not allowed in the central zone.

2. 2,3,7 & 11 of the red team are allowed inside the central zone but can only play passive defence.

3. 2,3,7 & 11 of the red team are allowed inside the central zone and are fully active.

4. The red team can tackle the white team players but are not allowed to intercept the ball when it is travelling.

5. The red team can play completely freely.

6. Only 1 goal for the white team to defend (the central goal).

Coaching Points

1. The correct angle and distance of the support player's positioning/movement is important in this exercise.

2. The wide forwards should make sharp movements inside to receive.

3. There should be a mixture of passes to feet and passes into space.

4. The final pass and the run in behind need to be very well coordinated to avoid being offside.

5. The 2 lines of 4 defenders need to work together when they press and try to block potential passes.

GOAL ANALYSIS
One Touch Combination Play with a 3rd Man Run

28-Jan-12

Real Madrid 3-1 Zaragoza (3rd Goal): Ozil - Assist: Kaka

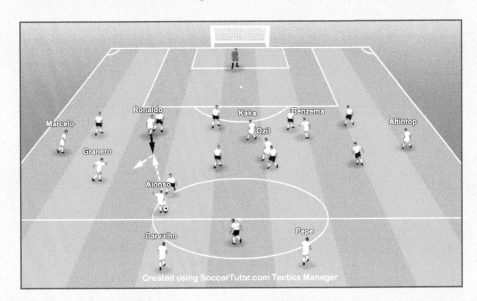

Alonso plays a vertical pass to Ronaldo. He is pressurised by the defender behind him so plays a pass back to Granero.

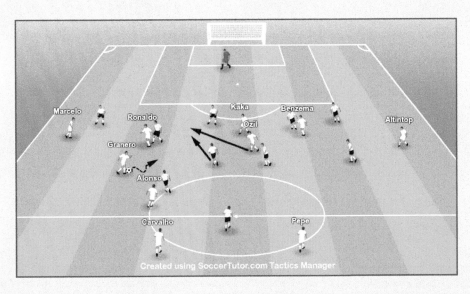

Granero dribbles the ball inside to disrupt the opposition's defensive shape and Ozil makes an opposite diagonal movement.

Granero passes to Kaka who plays a first time pass into space for Ozil to run onto (a 1-2 with a 3rd man run).

Ozil finishes the move by scoring the goal.

SESSION FOR THIS TOPIC *(5 Practices)*
1. Short and Long Passing Combination Play

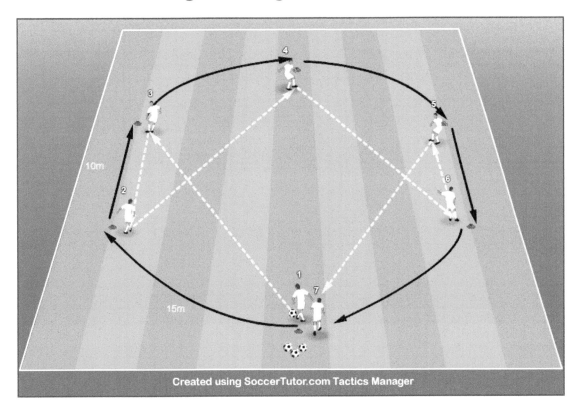

Created using SoccerTutor.com Tactics Manager

Objective
To develop a one touch passing game.

Description
In an area 30 yards x 30 yards we have 7 players and use 6 cones (1 at each end and 4 to the sides)

Start with one ball as player 1 passes to player 3. Player 3 passes to Player 2 who passes to player 4 and player 4 with one touch passes to Player 6. Player 6 passes to Player 5 and 5 passes back to the start position where Player 7 becomes Player 1. All players move to the next position after their pass (1 to 2, 2 to 3 etc).

Coaching Points
1. Players need to make sure their first touch is made on the move to maintain the fluency of the drill.
2. Reduce the time between the first touch and the pass, and then progress to 1 touch when possible.
3. Passes need to be weighted well and aimed just in front of their teammates to step forward up to.
4. The exercise should be done at a high tempo.

PROGRESSION

2. Quick Passing Combination, 3rd Man Run and Finish

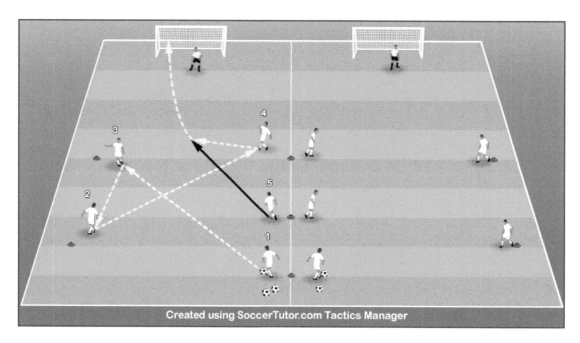

Created using SoccerTutor.com Tactics Manager

Objective

To develop one-two combinations with 3rd man runs.

Description

In an area 40 yards x 40 yards, divide the pitch into 2 zones. One group starts from the right and the other starts from the left. Both groups start in the 5 positions shown.

From Position 1 the player 1 (possible central defender or midfielder) passes to Player 3. Player 3 passes first time back to Player 2 and Player 2 makes a diagonal pass to player 4. While the ball is travelling, player 5 makes an opposite diagonal run into the space and receives the pass from player 4 and shoots at goal.

Coaching Points

1. The timing of the 3rd man run is the most important aspect here. This player needs to anticipate and start his run when the ball is travelling (as in the diagram) from player 2 to player 4.

2. The weight of the pass is key so the teammate can run onto the ball and is not slowed down.

3. Player 3's pass needs to be cushioned to take the pace off, allowing Player 2 to step up to the ball and play his pass.

PROGRESSION

3. Quick Combination, 3rd Man Run, Final Ball and Finish

Created using SoccerTutor.com Tactics Manager

Objective

To develop one-two combinations with 3rd man runs.

Description

Now we work with a functional practice, with central defenders or central midfielders, full backs, wide forwards, the attacking midfielder and the striker. The drill starts with the central defender (or midfielder) who makes a diagonal pass to the wide forward. The wide forward plays a first time pass to the left back (or central midfielder who is supporting on the side) who plays a pass into the striker. While the ball is travelling, the attacking midfielder makes an opposite diagonal movement and runs into the space behind the defensive line (mannequins) to receive the final ball from the striker and shoot at goal.

Coaching Points

1. All players need to create space (checking away) before moving to receive the pass.
2. The first pass should be accurate and fast aimed at feet. The second pass needs to be cushioned to take the pace off, allowing the next to step up to the ball and play his pass.
3. The player making the 3rd man run needs to anticipate and start his run when the ball is travelling to the striker.
4. The final pass and run in behind the defensive line need to be timed perfectly.

PROGRESSION

4. Through Balls & 3rd Man Runs in a Small Sided Game

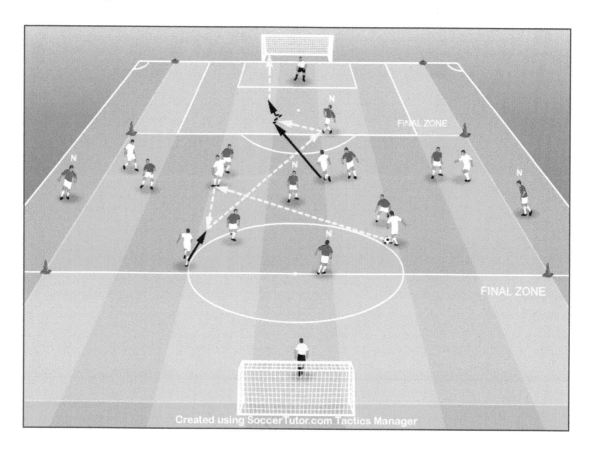

Objective

To develop one-two combinations with 3rd man runs.

Description 7 v 7 (+5 Neutral Players)

In an area 70 yards x 55 yards, we divide the pitch into 3 zones. The central zone is 55 yards x 34 yards and the 2 'Final Zones' are 55 yards x 18 yards. Both teams have 6 players inside the central zone in a 2-3-1 formation and 5 neutral players play with team in possession. To enter the 'Final Zone' the team in possession must play a 1-2 combination with a neutral player, with another making a 3rd man run to receive in behind and shoot at goal.

Rule Options

1. There are no defenders allowed in the 'Final Zones' but limited touches should be applied.

2. In the final zone the defenders are allowed but must be passive.

3. In the final zone, there must be 1 less defender than attacker. The attackers have limited touches.

4. In the final zone the defenders are fully active and there are unlimited touches.

Coaching Points

1. The corect angle and distance of the support player's positioning/movement is important in this exercise.

2. There should be a mixture of passes; to feet, into space and 1-2 combinations.

3. Players should make eye contact and be vocal when moving into space when they want to receive a pass

4. The timing of runs and passes into the final zone are key to success in this practice.

5. Shots should be taken quickly (first time if possible) and the focus should be on accuracy.

PROGRESSION

5. Quick Combinations & 3rd Man Runs in a 4 Zone Game

Objective

To develop one-two combinations with 3rd man runs.

Description 9 v 9

In half a full pitch we divide the area into 4 zones as shown. We have 4 goals; 2 full size goals in the centre and 2 mini goals either side of the goal on the halfway line. Both teams have 8 outfield players. The white team use a 2-2-3-1 formation (with 2 full backs, 2 central midfielders, 2 wide forwards, 1 attacking midfielder and 1 striker) and the other team (red) use a 4-4 formation.

Only the wide players (2,3,7 & 11 from both teams) are allowed in the side zones. To enter the 'Final Zone' the white team must play a 1-2 combination with another player making a 3rd man run to receive in behind the defensive line.

The other team can defend in the 'Final Zone' when the ball is played in there. The reds also try and score in any of the 3 goals, but they have limited touches or time to do this (6-8 passes or 8-10 seconds). If they score in the mini goals they get 1 point and if they score in the large goal they get 2 points.

Rule Options (Including Progressions)

1. 2,3,7 & 11 of the red team are not allowed in the central zone.

2. 2,3,7 & 11 of the red team are allowed inside the central zone but can only play passive defence.

3. 2,3,7 & 11 of the red team are allowed inside the central zone and are fully active.

4. The red team can tackle the white team players but are not allowed to intercept the ball when it is travelling.

5. The red team can play completely freely.

6. Only 1 goal for the white team to defend (the central goal).

Coaching Points

1. Use the same coaching points as in the previous practices on this topic.

2. Coach the correct positioning and distances of the support player.

3. Players should check away before moving to receive (to feet or in space).

GOAL ANALYSIS
3rd Man Overlapping Run & Final Ball Behind Defensive Line
4-Mar-12

Real Madrid 5-0 Espanyol (2nd Goal): Khedira - Assist: Ozil

Arbeloa dribbles the ball inside.

Arbeloa passes to Khedira in the centre. In front of the box we have a 5v5 with 1 support player on each side.

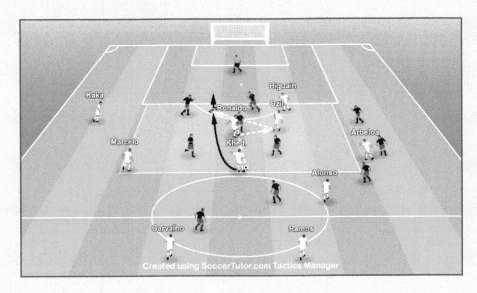

Khedira passes to Ronaldo and makes an overlapping run.

Ronaldo passes to Ozil and Ozil with one touch passes the ball into the path of an oncoming run from Khedira.

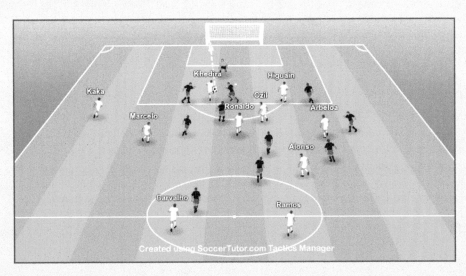

Khedira receives the ball inside the box and finishes at the near post to score.

SESSION FOR THIS TOPIC *(7 Practices)*

1. Dribble inside to Create Space for 3rd Man Overlap

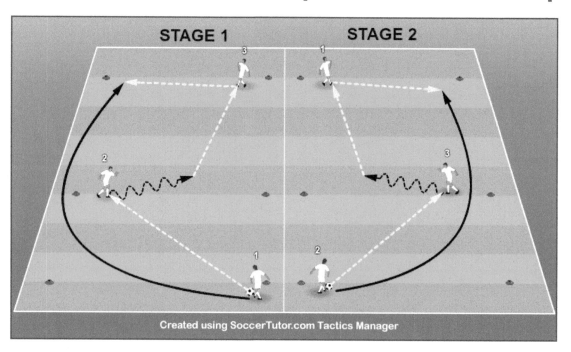

Created using SoccerTutor.com Tactics Manager

Objective

To develop one-two combinations with 3rd man runs.

Description

In an area 8 yards x 16 yards, we work with 3 players.

Stage 1 - The practice begins with Player 1 on the bottom right cone; he passes to Player 2 and then makes an overlapping run as shown. Player 2 dribbles inside and passes to Player 3 who uses a one touch to pass to player 1 who has made the overlapping run to receive.

Movements: Player 3 moves down to the right middle cone. Player 2 moves down to the left bottom cone. Player 1 makes a vertical pass to Player 2. The sequence can now start again from the bottom left cone.

Stage 2 - The sequence begins with Player 2 on the bottom left cone so the practice can be played from the opposite direction; he passes to Player 3 and then makes an overlapping run as shown. Player 3 dribbles inside and passes to Player 1 who makes a one touch pass to player 2 who has made the overlapping run to receive.

Coaching Points

1. The overlapping run should start as soon as the first player plays his pass.
2. The players need to communicate well for when to release the pass for the overlap so it is weighted perfectly and out in front of the player who is moving forward.
3. Player 2 should move sharply/quickly inside with his dribble (which creates room for the overlap).

PROGRESSION

2. Dribble Inside with 3ʳᵈ Man Overlap and Finish

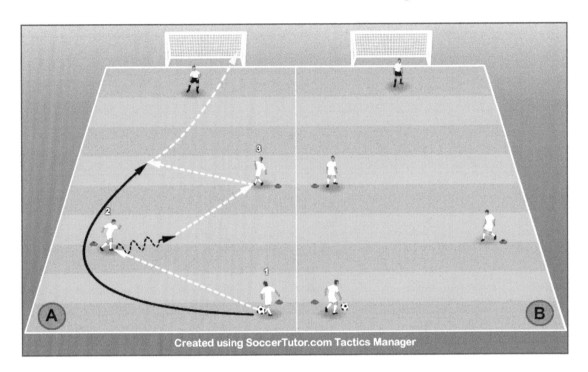

Created using SoccerTutor.com Tactics Manager

Description

We do the same practice, this time in front of goal with the overlapping run followed up with finishing past the goalkeeper.

This time we have 2 groups, one working from the left and the other from the right. All players should work from both sides during the practice.

Coaching Points

1. Players should practice finishing with both feet.

2. The finish should be with 1 touch when possible.

PROGRESSION

3. Combination, 3rd Man Overlap and Final Ball

Objective

To develop one-two combinations with 3rd man runs.

Description

Now we work within a functional practice, with central midfielders, full backs, wide forwards, an attacking midfielder and a striker.

The practice starts with the left back (3) who passes to the central midfielder (8). No.8 has moved forwards and passes to the attacking midfielder (10) before making an overlapping run around the back of him. No.10 passes to the striker (9) and the striker passes the ball first time in behind the defensive line where No.8 has continued his run into the space and can shoot at goal.

The sequence should then be repeated on the opposite side, starting with the right back's (2) pass to No.6.

Coaching Points

1. Player 3's pass should be hard and into the space for 8 to run onto.

2. The centre midfielder (8) should start his overlapping run as soon as he makes the pass to Player 10.

3. Player 9's final ball needs to be perfectly weighted and timed into the space for the overlapping run.

VARIATION

4. Dribble Inside, 3rd Man Overlap and Final Ball

Description

The variation again starts with the left back (3) who passes to the central midfielder (8). No.8 has moved forwards but this time he passes to the left forward (11) before making an overlapping run around the back of him. No.11 dribbles the ball inside and passes to the striker (9). The striker passes the ball first time in behind the defensive line where No.8 has continued his run into the space and can shoot at goal.

The sequence should then be repeated on the opposite side, starting with the right back's pass to No.6 (using the right forward (7) in the combination).

VARIATION 2

5. Dribble Inside, 3rd Man Overlap, Support and Final Pass

Description

The variation again starts with the left back (3) who passes to the central midfielder (8). No.8 has moved forwards and passes to the left forward (11) before making an overlapping run around the back of him. No.11 dribbles the ball inside and passes to the striker (9).

This time the striker is playing with his back to goal (as if under pressure from a defender behind him) and passes the ball first time back to the attacking midfielder (10) who plays the ball in behind the defensive line where No.8 has continued his run into the space and can shoot at goal.

The sequence should then be repeated on the opposite side, starting with the right back's pass to No.6 (using the right forward No.7 in the combination).

PROGRESSION

6. 3ʳᵈ Man Overlapping Runs with Side Zones in a SSG (1)

Objective

To develop one-two combinations with 3ʳᵈ man runs.

Description 7 v 7 (+5 Neutral Players)

In an area 70 yards x 55 yards we divide the pitch into 3 zones. The central zone is 55 yards x 34 yards and the 2 'Final Zones' are 55 yards x 18 yards. Both teams have 6 outfield players in a 2-3-1 formation with 5 neutral players playing with the team in possession. To enter the 'Final Zone' a player must receive the ball after making a 3ʳᵈ man overlapping run to receive in behind.

Rule Options

1. There are no defenders allowed in the 'Final Zones' but limited touches should be applied.

2. In the final zone the defenders are allowed but must be passive.

3. In the final zone, there must be 1 less defender than attacker. The attackers have limited touches.

4. In the final zone the defenders are fully active.

VARIATION

7. 3rd Man Overlapping Runs with Side Zones in a SSG (2)

Description 7 v 7 (+3 Neutral Players)

The only difference here is that we only have 3 neutrals players (instead of 5), 1 inside the central zone and 2 outside on the sides.

Coaching Points

1. The correct angle and distance of the support player's positioning/movement is important in this exercise.

2. There should be a mixture of passes; to feet, into space and 1-2 combinations.

3. Players should make eye contact and be vocal when moving into space when they want to receive a pass.

4. The timing of runs into the final zone are key to success in this practice.

5. Shots should be taken quickly (first time if possible) and the focus should be on accuracy.

GOAL ANALYSIS
1v1 on the Flank with Runs from the Centre into the Box (1)

22-Oct-11

Malaga 0-4 Real Madrid (2nd Goal): Ronaldo - Assist: Di Maria

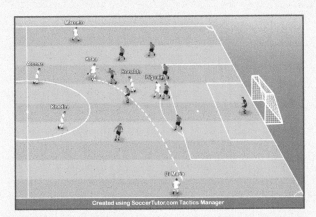

There are many players in the centre, so Kaka plays a long ball out wide to Di Maria and changes the direction of the game. The teammates leave Di Maria in the space.

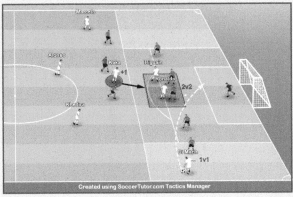

Di Maria is left 1v1 against the opposition full back and cuts in on his left foot and crosses the ball into the penalty area behind the defensive line towards Ronaldo, Higuain and Kaka.

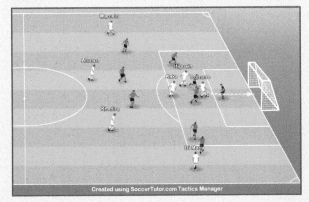

Now all players are attacking the space facing the goal. Ronaldo is the fastest and gets ahead of the defenders and finishes with 1 touch.

GOAL ANALYSIS

1v1 on the Flank with Runs from the Centre into the Box (2)

18-Mar-12

Real Madrid 1-1 Malaga: Benzema - Assist: Ronaldo

Kaka passes to Ronaldo on the flank and the other Real Madrid players leave him the space to play 1v1 on the left side.

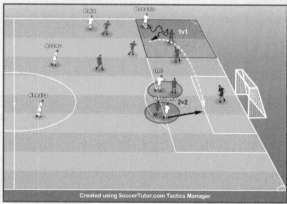

Ronaldo uses his good dribbling technique and changes direction to the right, then crosses the ball round the back of the defensive line. Ozil makes a run to the near post and Benzema makes a run to the far post.

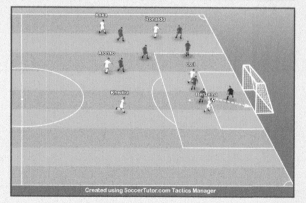

Benzema heads in at the back post.

GOAL ANALYSIS
1v1 on the Flank with Runs from the Centre into the Box (3)
31-Mar-12
Osasuna 1-5 Real Madrid (5th Goal): Higuain - Assist: Ronaldo

The ball is with Ronaldo on the left side and his teammates leave him the space again.

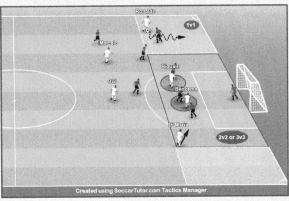

Ronaldo has a 1v1 situation on the left and the other Madrid players make runs into the box; one near post (Higuain), one far post (Benzema) and a 3rd coming in from the right (Di Maria). This creates a 2v2 or 3v3 situation in the box.

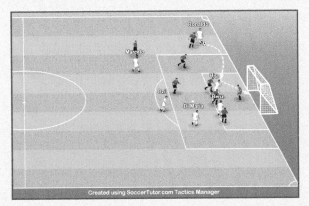

Ronaldo crosses the ball to the near post and Higuain scores a goal with his head.

SESSION FOR THIS TOPIC *(6 Practices)*
1. Timing of Runs with Short Crossing and Finishing

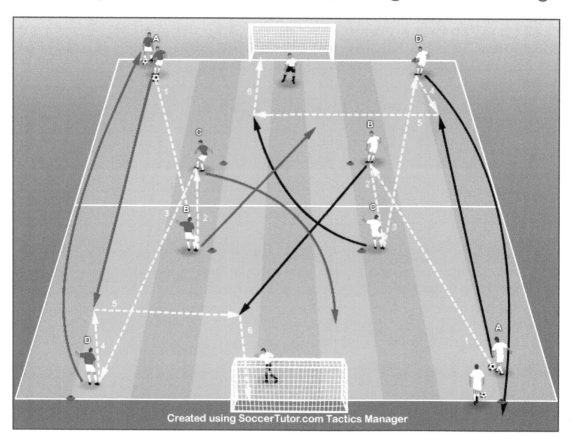

Created using SoccerTutor.com Tactics Manager

Objective

To develop crossing and finishing (with combination play).

Description

In an area 40 yards x 40 yards, we use 2 goals and we have 6 starting positions with 12 players. 2 players are positioned on the right at each end, 1 to the left at each end, 4 in the centre and we have 2 Goalkeepers.

The drill starts with 2 balls from the 2 player A's. They both pass the ball to the player facing them (B). These players play a first time short pass to the other centre player (C), who then passes to Player D at the other end. Player A makes a run as soon as he passed the ball earlier to receive first time from Player D and crosses the ball across the face of goal. Both Player C's make a curved run to opposite goals at the back post. Both Player B's run to the near post of opposite goals to finish past the goalkeeper.

The players then change positions to start the practice again. (A and D on the same side swap, the 2 Player B's swap positions, as do the Player C's). The exercise should also be switched to cross from the left side.

Coaching Points

1. This practice requires a mix of passes - long passes to feet, short cushioned passes and passes into space across the face of goal.

2. Players should check away from their cone and then move to receive the pass, which creates space making it easier for the players to play with 1 touch.

3. The timing of the passes and the runs needs to be the same from both sides for the practice to flow properly.

4. The final ball and the run to the near or far post should be coordinated to allow good first time finishes.

PROGRESSION
2. Switching Play and Crossing in a Position Specific Practice

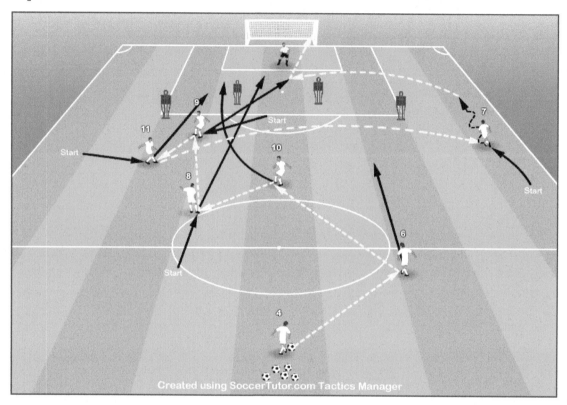

Description

Using 2/3 of a full pitch, we place 4 mannequins in defensive positions as shown. We have players in 7 positions from the 4-2-3-1. We have 1 central defender with all the midfielders and attackers.

The central defender (4) passes to the central midfielder (6). No.6 makes a direct pass into the feet of the attacking midfielder (10) who passes first time to the other central midfielder (8). The striker (9) supports and receives the ball from No.8. The striker passes first time to No.11 who has made an inside run to change the direction of play to the right flank and plays a long pass to the right forward (7). No.7 dribbles the ball down the line and crosses into the box.

4 players make their runs into the box. The striker runs to the near post and No.10 runs to the far post. The other 2 players arrive later; one behind them (8) and one coming in from the other side (11).

Coaching Points

1. Players should check away from their starting positions and then move to receive the pass.
2. The players should take up the correct positions and distances in their support play.
3. When Player 11 changes the direction of play, the pass must be accurate and be played for 7 to run onto.
4. The rhythm and timing of the movement and passing needs to be monitored again.

PROGRESSION
3. 1v1 on the Flanks: Crossing & Finishing with Side Zones

Objective

To develop 1v1 play on the flank, crossing, finishing and timing runs into the penalty area.

Description

Using half a full size pitch, divide the area into 3 zones as shown with a length double the size of the box (36 yards). In the central area we play 2v2 and in the side areas we play 1v1.

The central midfielder (8) starts with the ball and passes either to the left or the right side (blue 6 is a passive defender). The wide forwards (7 or 11) who are in the 1v1 area have the objective to beat the defender and cross the ball into the penalty area for their teammates to score. In the centre there is a 2v2 situation created as attackers look to score and the defenders try to prevent them. White 8 makes a run forward followed by a passive defender (blue 6) which creates a 3v2 (+1) situation.

Different rules: 1) The blue defenders are passive. **2)** The blue centre backs are passive, but the full backs are active. **3)** All the blue players are fully active.

Coaching Points

1. Players should check away from the defenders before moving to receive a pass or find space in the penalty area.
2. Good dribbling and close control is needed in the side zones to win the 1v1.
3. The attackers need to show good timing with their runs into the box so they can finish first time.
4. The attackers need to communicate so that 1 player makes a run to the near post, and the other to the far post.
5. Accurate crossing and finishing is needed to score goals under pressure.

VARIATION

4. 1v1 in the Centre and on the Flanks with Side Zones

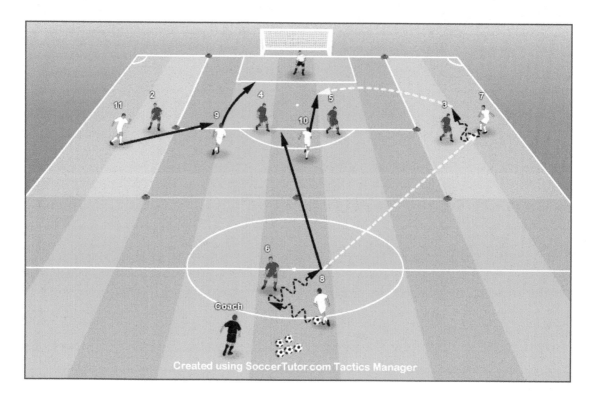

Description

Here we show a variation of the same drill with 2 important differences.

1. The blue defender (6) is fully active and aims to prevent No.8 passing to the flanks.

2. This time, when one wide forward crosses into the box, the wide forward on the opposite side (number 11 in the example shown) also makes a run into the box to try and score.

Different rules

1. The blue team's full back is not allowed in the central zone.

2. The blue team's full back is allowed in the central zone.

PROGRESSION

5. 2v2 on the Flanks - Crossing & Finishing with Side Zones

Description

Using half a pitch, we mark out 3 zones as shown. We have 1 mini goal in each side zone. In the central zone we have 2v2 (attacking midfielder & striker vs 2 central defenders). In the side zones we have 2v2 (full back & wide forward vs full back & winger).

The drill starts in one of the side zones. The side players must lose their marker and receive a pass from the coach. The white team must work to find solutions to get the ball forwards and through the end of the zone where one of them has 1 or 2 touches to cross the ball into the penalty area for the 3 players making runs. The defenders are not allowed to follow the attacking players out of the zone.

The defenders from the opposite side are not allowed in the centre. If the 2 blue defenders win the ball in the side zone they have 6 seconds to score in the mini goal (and the whites must quickly make the transition from attack to defence).

VARIATION

6. 2v2 on the Flanks - Switching Play, Crossing & Finishing

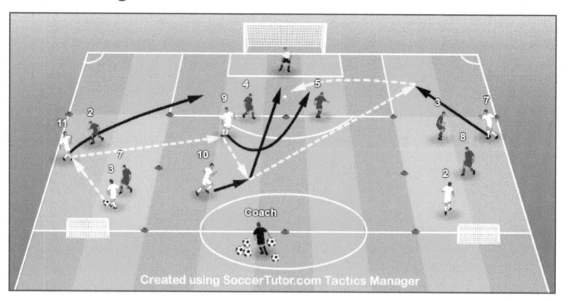

Description

Here the objective of the 2 side players is to pass the ball to the striker. The striker then plays a first time pass to No.10 who switches the play, passing into the space in behind for the wide forward (7) on the other side to cross for the 3 players making runs into the box.

GOAL ANALYSIS
Intelligent Positioning in the Box with Quick Finishing

28-Aug-11

Zaragoza 0-6 Real Madrid (3rd Goal): Alonso

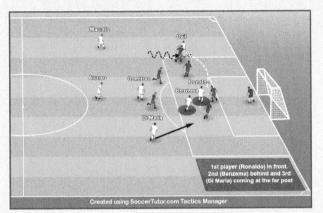

Ozil dribbles past the right back and crosses into the penalty area. Real again have 1 player (Ronaldo) at the near post, Benzema behind him and the 3rd (Di Maria) makes a run to the far post.

There are also 3 players outside of the box for 2 reasons - firstly to win the potential second ball and secondly to be the first line of defence for a possible transition.

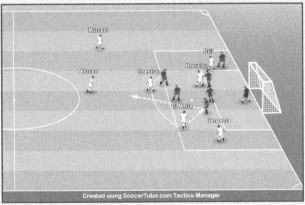

The ball reaches Di Maria and his shot is blocked by the defender. There are too many players inside the box (6 from the opposition and 4 from Real).

The ball bounces outside the area where Real have good balance and Alonso is in a lot of space.

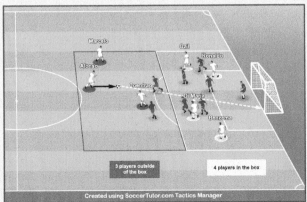

Alonso, who moves forward towards the ball hits his shot first time and scores from long distance.

SESSION FOR THIS TOPIC *(3 Practices)*
1. Quick Finishing in and Around the Penalty Area

Created using SoccerTutor.com Tactics Manager

Objective

To develop attacking combinations and quick finishing inside and outside of the penalty area.

Description 7 v 5

We use an area double the size of the penalty box and have 2 full size goals. The white team uses a 2-3-1 formation and the blues are in a 2-2 formation. In 1 grid, we have 3v2 (the central midfield players). In the other grid we have a 1v2 with 1 white striker and 2 blue central defenders. The wide forwards for the white team are free to move all the way along each side, but must not enter the main playing area.

The objective for the white team is to use high tempo combinations and creative attacking play inside and outside of the box to score (they must use the wide forwards). The drill always starts with the white goalkeeper and the white team are limited to 1 or 2 touches. If the blue team score it counts double.

Coaching Points

1. This practice should be played at a high tempo.

2. Good and quick decision making is required for this attacking combination play practice.

3. Encourage creativity and shots from inside or outside the penalty area.

4. Good short crosses should be accurate and timed/weighted for the run.

5. Players need to be prepared to react very quickly to a transition from defence to attack or vice versa.

PROGRESSION

2. Transition Play - Winning the 2nd Ball with Quick Finishing

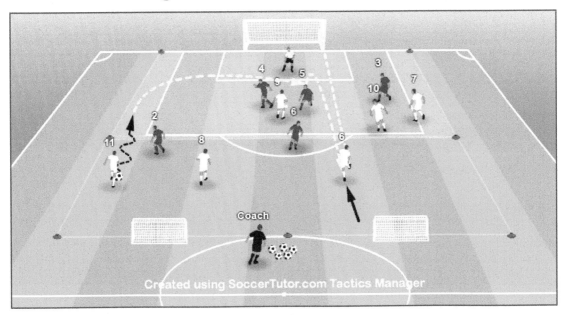

Objective

To develop attacking combinations and quick finishing inside and outside of the penalty area. To work on winning the second ball and transitions from attack to defence high up the pitch.

Description 6 v 5 (+GK)

Here we work in the the final 3rd of the pitch. Divide the area into 2 zones as shown. We have 1 full size goal and 2 mini goals. The white team uses the 2-3-1 formation and the blue team are using a 4-1 formation.

The white team starts with the ball and attacks the one goal. The blue team defend deep inside and outside the box. The white team always keep 2 players in their own half for the second ball and to prepare for a defensive transition. If the blue team win the ball, they try to score in the 2 mini goals with a maximum of 5-6 touches. When the ball goes out, the coach passes a new ball to the white team to start again.

Coaching Points

1. Without the side players from the previous practice, encourage players to dribble the ball, beating their direct opponent in 1v1 situations.

2. If the white team lose the ball, they need to close down the player in possession immediately to prevent the blues scoring in the mini goals (great practice for game situations - preventing a player from turning and making a forward pass).

3. The 2 white central midfielders must try to win the second ball and shoot from distance.

VARIATION

3. Winning the Ball Back Immediately in a Dynamic Game

Description 6 v 6 (+GK)

Here we combine the 2 zones to make 1 large playing area. This time, we have 3 mini goals, 1 in the centre and 2 at the sides. The 2 side mini goals should be angled to face the blue players. The blue team also now have an extra central midfield player.

The white players again try to combine to score, but if they lose possession they must close down the blue players immediately to prevent them scoring in the mini goals.

If the blue team scores in the side mini goal they get 1 point and if they score in the central mini goal they get 2 points. When the ball goes out, the coach immediately passes a new ball to the white team and they start again.

GOAL ANALYSIS
Full Back's In Advanced Positions: Crossing and Finishing
13-May-12

Real Madrid 4-1 Mallorca (1st Goal): Ronaldo - Assist: Marcelo

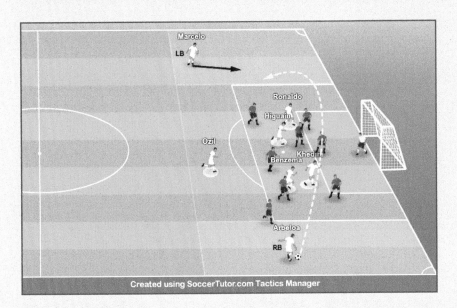

The opponent again has many players inside the penalty area. Arbeloa delivers the cross from the right flank. 4 players from Real Madrid and 7 from the opponent are in the box but the ball goes over their heads and onto the left flank.

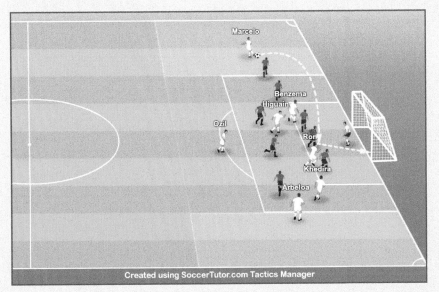

Marcelo (the left back) crosses to the far post. Real have 4 players close to goal with good positions (distances) and Ronaldo displays his heading ability scoring at the back post.

SESSION FOR THIS TOPIC *(2 Practices)*
1. Crossing and Finishing with Advanced Full Backs (1)

Objective

To develop attacking and defensive play inside the penalty area.

Description 8 v 6 (+GK)

In the final third of the pitch we mark out 3 zones as shown in the diagram. We have 1 full size goal and 2 mini goals at the other end. The white team have their 2 full backs in the side zones and the blue team is in a 4-2 formation.

The white team starts with the ball and attacks, trying to score from inside or outside the box. The white team's 2 full backs have to stay in the outside zones and they are limited to 2 touches. You can either allow no blue defending players in the side zones or limit it to 1 player at a time.

If the blue team win possession they try to score in the 2 mini goals with a maximum of 5 touches. When the ball goes out of play, the coach immediately passes a new ball in to the white team to start again.

Coaching Points

1. The use of attacking width on the flank is the key to this practice to produce quality crosses and quick finishing.
2. Decision making, accuracy and weight of pass, positioning in the box and timing of runs are all important.
3. Encourage the players to communicate and be creative with their attacking combinations.
4. Quick reactions to losing the ball are needed (transition play) - winning the second ball.

VARIATION

2. Crossing and Finishing with Advanced Full Backs (2)

Description 8 v 6(+GK)

We use the same pitch area, but the 2 side zones are now reduced to the length of the penalty area. This time there are 4 mini goals. The 2 white full backs now work in the wide area next to the penalty area. The blue team are not allowed to enter the side zones.

The blue team aim to score in the 4 mini goals when the white team's attack breaks down or the ball is cleared (the white team are then in transition from attack to defence).

When the ball goes out of play, the coach immediately passes a new ball in to the white team to start again.

GOAL ANALYSIS
Switching Play to Change the Point of Attack (1)

28-Aug-11

Zaragoza 0-6 Real Madrid (2nd Goal): Marcelo - Assist: Ramos

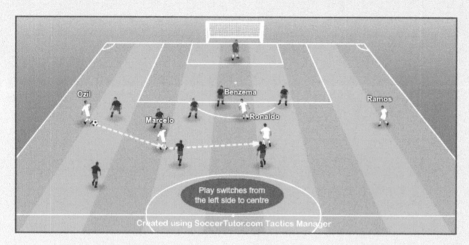

Real Madrid attack against an organised ball oriented defence. Using the width of the pitch. Real Madrid switch the play to the weak side of the opposition. Ozil passes to Marcelo, who with his first touch passes inside to Ronaldo.

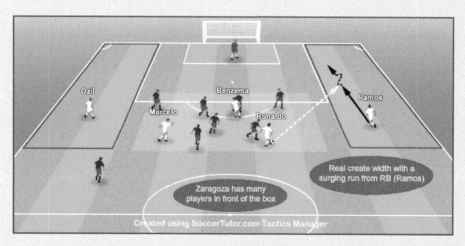

Ronaldo plays a pass out wide to Ramos who has made a run up the right flank. The opposition have many players (strong organisation) in the centre, and leave free space near the sidelines.

Ramos receives the ball in the free space on the right flank and crosses into the box. Real have one player at the near post (Benzema), one behind him (Ronaldo), one coming from the other side at the far post (Ozil), and a 4th player (Marcelo) coming in at the back.

Marcelo takes a very good first touch and takes the ball onto his stronger foot and with his second touch strikes the ball into the side of the net.

GOAL ANALYSIS
Switching Play to Change the Point of Attack (2)

28-Aug-11

Zaragoza 0-6 Real Madrid (6ᵗʰ Goal): Ronaldo - Assist: Kaka

Here we have the same situation, but the play starts from the right. Ramos dribbles the ball inside and causes the opposition defence to become imbalanced. Kaka makes a run in the opposite direction (diagonal). Ramos passes inside to Alonso.

Alonso dribbles past his direct opponent to work a position and pass to the free player (Kaka).

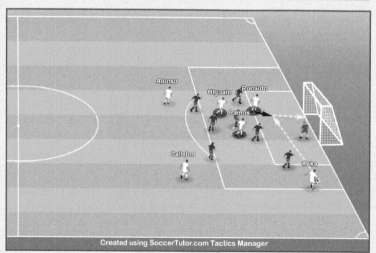

Kaka receives the ball from Alonso and puts in a low cross behind the defensive line. Real have 3 players in the box again. They are at good distances and have a good shape (with 2 players outside the box). Ronaldo scores the goal.

GOAL ANALYSIS
Switching Play to Change the Point of Attack (3)

05-May-11

Granada 1-2 Real Madrid (2ⁿᵈ Goal): Own Goal - Assist: Benzema

Callejon dribbles the ball towards the defenders. Granada have 6 players close together in the centre. When the defenders close down the ball carrier, Callejon waits for the correct timing and passes to Benzema who is free in space on the right flank.

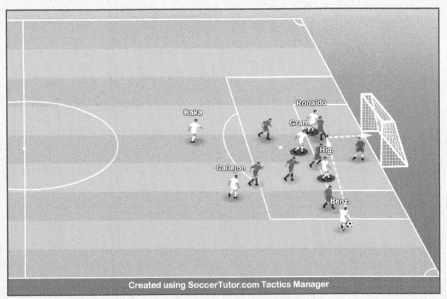

Benzema plays a low cross behind the defensive line, so all players (defenders and attackers) are facing the goal. There is a touch and an own goal from the Granada defender. 3 Madrid players again keep good positions and shape in the box (near post, far post, behind + 2 outside of the box).

GOAL ANALYSIS
Switching Play to Change the Point of Attack (4)

28-Jan-12
Real Madrid 3-1 Zaragoza (2ⁿᵈ Goal): Ronaldo - Assist: Ozil

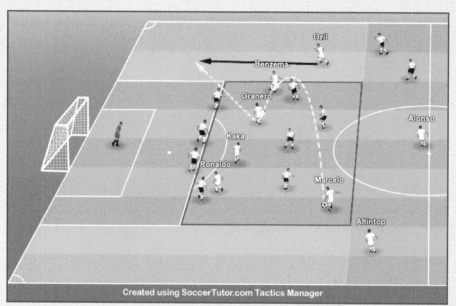

8 Zaragoza players are in the central area using a 2 zone defence. Marcelo plays a lofted pass behind the midfield line to Benzema, who with one touch passes inside to Granero. Granero is under pressure from the defenders and passes into the free space on the right for Ozil's oncoming run.

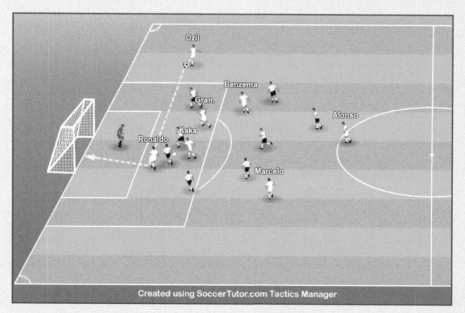

Ozil hits a cross first time round the back of the defensive line (all players are again facing the goal). Ronaldo finishes with 1 touch to score.

SESSION FOR THIS TOPIC *(4 Practices)*

1. Utilising Width and Switching Play in a Small Sided Game

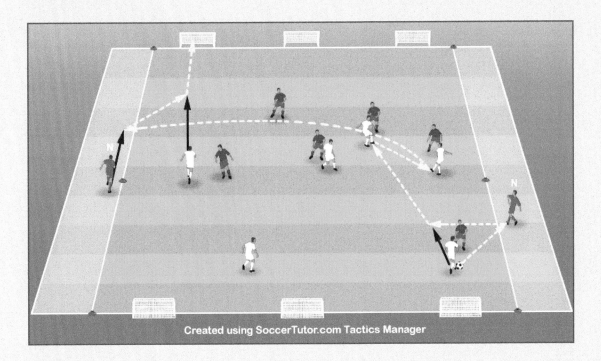

Created using SoccerTutor.com Tactics Manager

Objective

To develop possession play and utilising the full width of the pitch to attack. We also develop switching of play and changing the point of attack.

Description 6 v 6 (+2 Neutral Players)

In an area 50 yards x 40 yards, we divide the pitch into 3 zones. The central zone is 40 yards x 40 yards. The 2 side zones are both 40 yards x 5 yards. In the central zone, we have 6 mini goals (3 at each end) and a 6v6 situation with both teams using the 2-3-1 formation. At the sides, we have 2 neutral players who play with the team in possession. Only the neutral players are allowed in the side zones and they are not allowed in the centre.

The aim for the teams is to complete 8 passes (1 point). If they score in any of the 3 mini goals when they are attacking they get 2 points. If a player scores directly from a pass from a neutral player they get 3 points.

Different rules: 1) The Neutral Players can score. **2)** The Neutral Players cannot score. **3)** All players have unlimited touches and must finish with 1 touch. **4)** Limit all players to 2-3 touches and must finish with 1 touch.

Coaching Points

1. Encourage the players to quickly change the direction of attack by switching play to the wide neutral players.
2. There should be caution on the ball (less risk) so the team maintain possession for the switch of play.

PROGRESSION

2. Switching Play with Advanced Full Backs in a SSG (1)

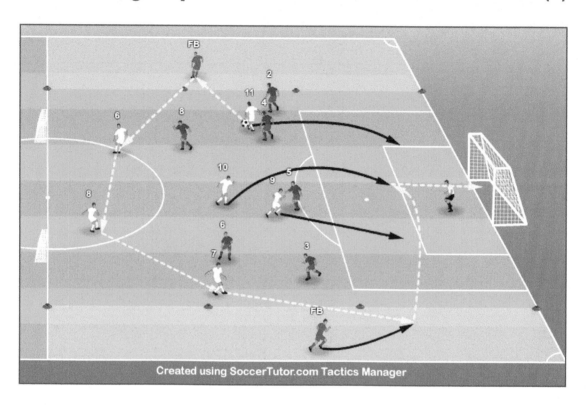

Created using SoccerTutor.com Tactics Manager

Description 6 (+2 Full Backs) v 6 (+GK)

Using half a full size pitch, we divide the area into 3 zones as shown. 1 team defends a full size goal and the other team defend 2 mini goals. In the central zone we have a 6v6 situation with the white team in a 2-3-1 formation and the blue team are using a 4-2 formation (+ a goalkeeper). In the sides zones (where the central players are not allowed) we have 2 full backs who play with the white team in possession.

If a white player scores directly from a pass from a full back the goal counts double. If the blue team win the ball and score in either of the 2 mini goals, it also counts as double. The teams change roles and the coach keeps record of the score.

Different rules: 1) Full backs can come inside and score. **2)** Full Backs can come inside but cannot score. **3)** Full Backs are always outside. **4)** Unlimited touches and finish with 1 touch. **5)** Maximum of 2-3 touches and finish with 1 touch.

Coaching Points

1. The tempo of the play should be high with quick passing and movement.

2. The attacking players need to have good starting positions around the box and time their runs inside to meet the crosses making sure to attack different areas (communication).

3. Both teams need to be prepared for a possible transition and react quickly when the situation changes.

VARIATION

3. Switching Play with Advanced Full Backs in a SSG (2)

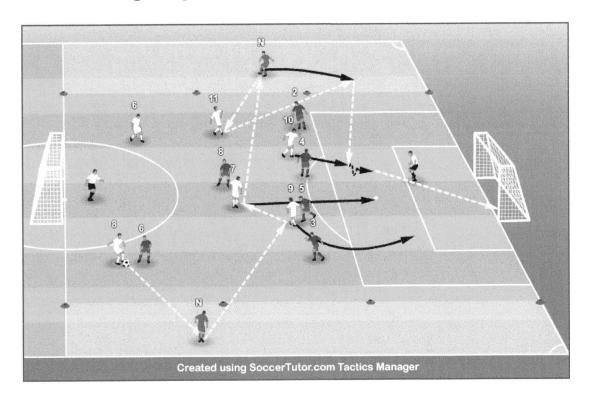

Created using SoccerTutor.com Tactics Manager

Description 7 v 7 (+2 Neutral Players)

In this progression, both teams defend a full size goal.

When in possession, both teams use a 2-3-1 formation and when defending both use a 4-2 formation.

Both teams are able to use the 2 neutral players in the side zones when they are in possession.

Different rules

1. Neutrals can come inside and score.

2. Neutrals can come inside but cannot score.

3. Neutrals are always outside.

4. Unlimited touches and finish with 1 touch.

5. Maximum of 2-3 touches and finish with 1 touch.

PROGRESSION

4. Using Width and Creating Space in and Around the Box

Objective

The aim for the white team is to develop their attacking combinations against opponents who are using a ball oriented defensive strategy with a lot of bodies in a central area.

Description 6 v 5 (+GK)

Approximately 10 yards to 15 yards outside the penalty area, place 5 cones as shown. Divide the area into 3 zones as displayed in the diagram. 3 yards away from the side zones and 5 yards from the centre, put 3 mini goals outside of the playing area. The white team uses a 2-3-1 formation and the blues use a 4-1 formation.

The drill starts when the coach passes to a white player. The white team aim to score. If the blues win the ball they must aim to score in the 3 mini goals (quick transition from defence to attack). If a goal is scored or the ball goes out of play, the coach on the other side immediately passes a new ball in to a player on the white team.

Coaching Points

1. The white team players must utilise dribbling up the pitch to draw defenders onto them, so they can then pass into space for their teammates to exploit.

2. If the defenders maintain their balance and there is a lack options, the white team should look to change the direction of play quickly to the weak side of the opponent.

GOAL ANALYSIS
Timed Runs in Between the Full Back and Centre Back (1)

06-Nov-11

Real Madrid 7-1 Osasuna (5ᵗʰ Goal): Ronaldo - Assist: Arbeloa

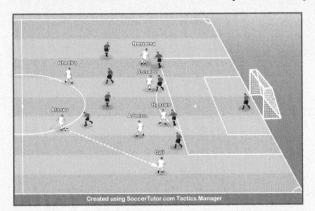

Alonso passes to Ozil on the right side and takes the whole Osasuna midfield out of the game (neutralises them).

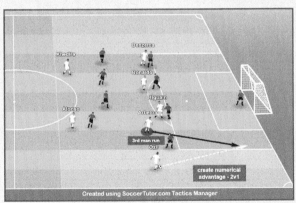

Arbeloa makes a diagonal run between the left back and the central defender (which creates a numerical advantage of 2v1). Ozil passes at the correct time into the space in behind and neutralises the second defensive line (the back 4).

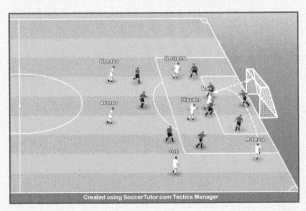

Arbeloa crosses the ball into the centre of the box with Ronaldo, Benzema and Higuain making runs into the penalty area. Ronaldo scores the goal with a header.

GOAL ANALYSIS
Timed Runs in Between the Full Back and Centre Back (2)

18-Feb-12

Real Madrid 4-0 Racing Santander (1st Goal): Ronaldo - Assist: Kaka

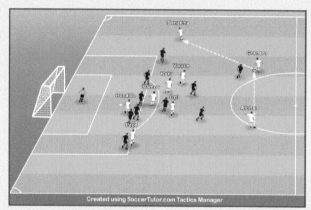

A very similar situation occurs here. Granero passes to Benzema on the right side. There are 6 Racing Santander players in line with the edge of the penalty area.

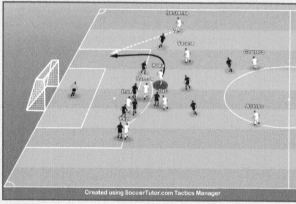

Kaka makes a horizontal movement and then makes a cutting vertical run in between the left back and central defender. Benzema passes at the correct time into the space for Kaka to run onto.

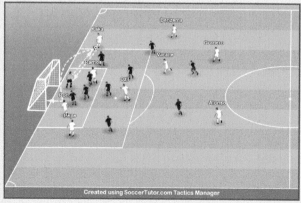

Kaka's first cross is blocked, but with his second attempt he delivers his cross to the back post where again Ronaldo heads in to score the goal. Pepe, Ramos, Ozil were also all inside the box.

SESSION FOR THIS TOPIC *(3 Practices)*
1. Passing in Behind the Defensive Line in a 9 Zone SSG

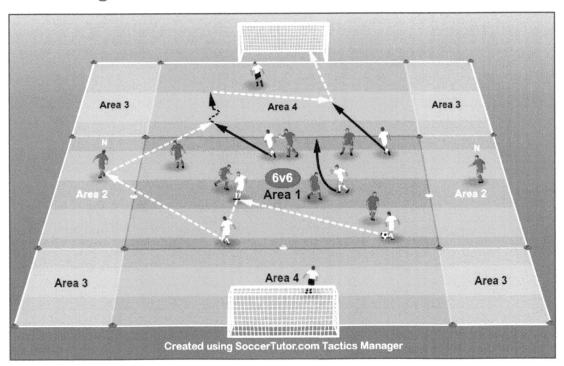

Created using SoccerTutor.com Tactics Manager

Objective
To develop team play attacking in behind the defensive line; making runs in between the full back and the central defender when the opponent defends with a deep line.

Description 7 v 7 (+2 Neutral Players)
In an area 60 yards x 55 yards, we divide the pitch into 9 zones. The central area is 35 yards x 40 yards. The 'Area 2s' are 35 yards x 7.5 yards, the 'Area 3s' are 12.5 yards x 7.5 yards and the 'Area 4s' are 12. 5 yards x 40 yards.

In area 1, we play 6v6 and the team in possession can play with the 2 neutrals players (who are in area 2s). The neutral players must stay in area 2 and only 1 defender can go in there at a time. The attacking team tries to find solutions to create chances, taking advantage of the neutral players and making diagonal runs (cuts) into areas 3 and 4.

Different rules: 1) No marking in area 3, but attackers limited to 2 touches. **2)** Allow marking in area. **3)** Use unlimited touches in area 1 and limit th e touches in the other areas. **4)** Maximum of 2-3 touches, but must finish with 1 touch.

Coaching Points
1. Correct body shape (open up on the half turn) and positioning is important to view where the options for where the next pass is going.
2. The correct angles and distance of supporting players from the man in possession are key to provide options.
3. The timing of the pass and the run need to be coordinated (communication), as well as quality finishing.

PROGRESSION

2. Exploiting Space in Behind with Diagonal Runs in a SSG

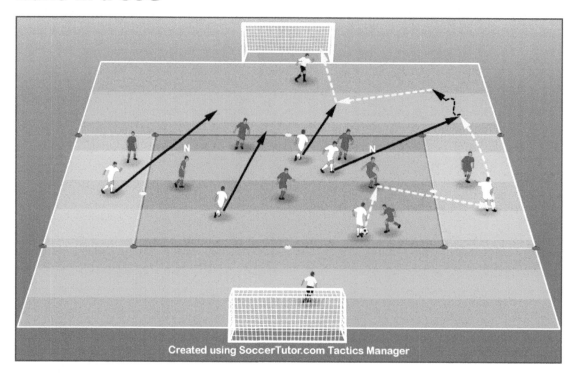

Created using SoccerTutor.com Tactics Manager

Description 7 v 7 (+2 Neutral Players)

Here we combine areas 3 and 4 and put the 2 neutrals players into the central zone. Each team is allowed one player in both size zones at a time. The defenders can mark the attackers in the end zones.

Different rules:

1. Neutral players can score goals

2. Neutral players are not allowed to score.

3. Players have unlimited touches (neutral players limited to 2 touches) and finishing is limited to 1 touch.

4. Limit the players to 2-3 touches (neutral players limited to 1 touch) and finishing is limited to 1 touch.

PROGRESSION

3. Timing Runs in Between Defenders Who Use a Deep Line

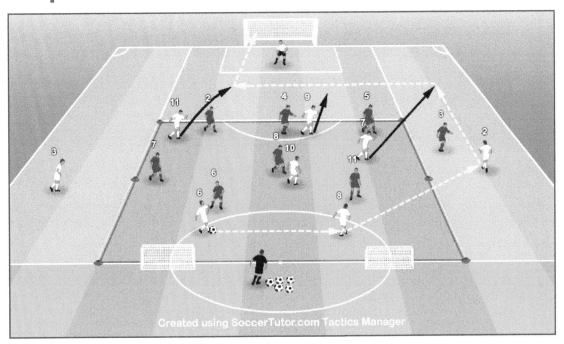

Created using SoccerTutor.com Tactics Manager

Objective

To develop team play attacking in behind the defensive line; making runs in between the full back and the central defender when the opponent defends with a deep line.

Description 8 v 8 (+GK)

Using half a full size pitch, we divide the area into 1 central zone and 2 side zones (channels). The central zone is split into 2 grids at the edge of the penalty area as shown. We place 2 mini goals on the halfway line. The white team is using a 2-2-3-1 formation (2 full backs, 2 central midfielders, 1 attacking midfielder, 2 side forwards and 1 striker). The other team is using a 4-4 formation.

Only 1 blue player can enter the side zones at a time, so the white team can create a numerical advantage (2v1) in these side zones. The blue team try to win the ball and then score in the mini goals which count as double. If the white team lose possession they must make a quick transition from attack to defence.

Different rules:

1. The white players in the central zone have limited touches, but are unlimited at the sides.
2. The white players in the central zone have unlimited touches and are limited to 2-3 touches at the sides.
3. Limited touches for all players but the blue team have limited time or touches to finish their attack.
4. All players including the blue team have unlimited touches and time.

GOAL ANALYSIS
Attacking in Behind the Defensive Line Through the Centre

17-Dec-11

Sevilla 2-6 Real Madrid (2nd Goal): Callejon - Assist: Di Maria

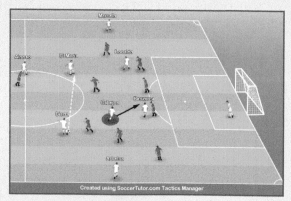

Diarra makes a pass inside to Di Maria. There is a well organised defence in front of him. Callejon recognises the situation and moves forward.

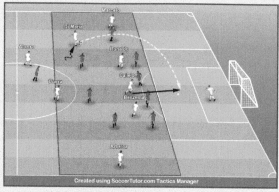

Callejon makes a run in between the 2 central defenders. Di Maria demonstrates excellent vision and decision making, playing a lofted pass behind the defensive line and neutralises all 8 defensive players of the opposition.

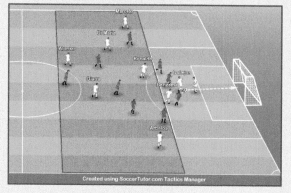

The pass is perfectly timed for Callejon to run onto and score past the goalkeeper.

SESSION FOR THIS TOPIC *(4 Practices)*
1. 6v6 (+2) Passing into the 'Goal Zone' Small Sided Game

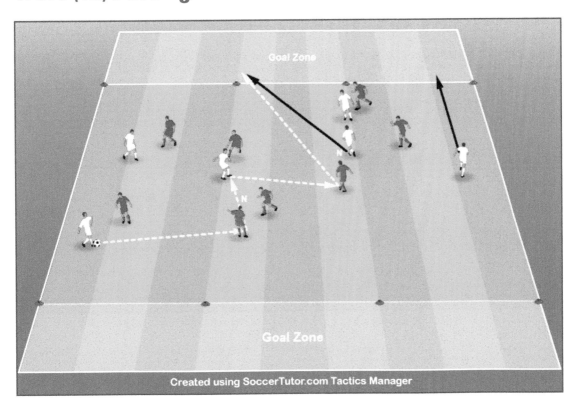

Created using SoccerTutor.com Tactics Manager

Objective

To develop the ability to attack in behind the defensive line - quality and timing of run and final pass.

Description 6 v 6 (+2 Neutral Players)

In an area 45 yards x 40 yards we divide the pitch into 3 zones. The central zone is 35 yards x 40 yards and the goal zones are both 5 yards x 40 yards. We have a 6v6 and 2 neutral players who play with the team in possession. The 2 neutral players act as central midfielders in the 4-2-3-1 formation. The other players take up the other positions (2 full backs, 2 wide forwards, an attacking midfielder and a striker).

The objective for the team in possession is to find solutions and use quick combinations to get the ball into the goal zone (in behind the defensive line). To get a point, the team in possession must play a pass into the 'Goal Zone' and a teammate must receive the ball under full control.

Coaching Points

1. With a numerical advantage, the attacking team should have players making runs into the space behind often.

2. Key aspects: Speed and quality of pass, good decision making, correct angles and distances for support play and creative combination play and movement.

PROGRESSION

2. 6v6 (+2) Support Play in a 1v1 Zonal Dynamic Game

Created using SoccerTutor.com Tactics Manager

Description 7 v 7 (+2 Neutral Players)

Now we divide the playing area into 6 grids (about 10 yards x 10 yards each). In each grid we have a 1v1 situation and we still have the 2 neutral players who play with the team in possession. The normal players are only allowed in their own grid, unless they are making a run into the 'Goal Zone'. The neutral players are free to move anywhere and they help to create numerical advantages with the team in possession (2v1 or 3v1).

Rule: Unlimited touches for the normal players and a maximum of 1-2 touches for the neutral players.

Coaching Points

1. Players need to protect the ball in these 1v1 situations; shielding the ball from their direct opponent.

2. Strength is needed to prevent the defending players from winning the ball (getting your body in between the opponent and the ball.

3. The neutral players are responsible for playing 1-2 combinations and making 3rd man runs to progress the attack.

PROGRESSION

3. 7v7 (+2) Runs in Behind and Finishing in a SSG

Objective

To develop the ability to attack in behind the defensive line - quality and timing of run and final pass.

Description 7 v 7 (+2 Neutral Players)

In an area 75 yards x 40 yards, we divide the pitch into 3 zones. The central zone is 35 yards x 40 yards and the end zones are both 20 yards x 40 yards. The team in possession use a 2-2-3-1 formation (with 2 neutral players). After a team has made a minimum number of passes (coaches discretion) they look to play a final ball into the end zone for an attacking player (teammate) to run onto.

Different rules: 1) Players can play the final ball without a minimum of passes required before. 2) No defenders allowed in the end zones and the attackers have a maximum of 2 touches to score. 3) Allow 1 defender and 2 attackers in the end zone at a time. 4) The attacking team are limited to 2 touches and can only score with a 1 touch finish. 5) All players can enter the end zone when the ball is played in there.

Coaching Points

1. At first the aim is to keep possession and utilise the numerical advantage and all the space available.

2. After a minimum amount of passes is achieved, encourage a quick transition with forward passing and forward runs to get in behind and score as quickly as possible.

3. The rhythm and timing of the movement/runs is key to good attacking combinations.

PROGRESSION

4. Receiving in Behind the Defensive Line - 9v9

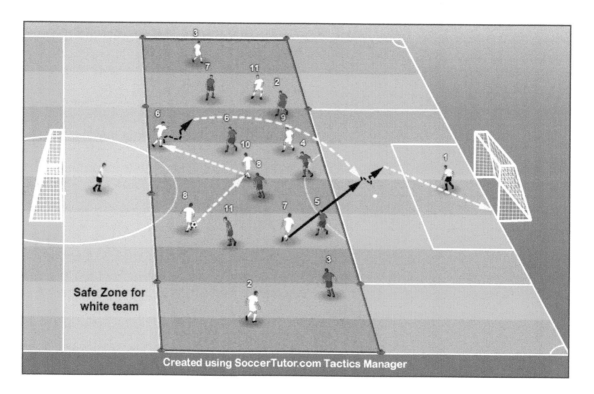

Safe Zone for white team

Created using SoccerTutor.com Tactics Manager

Objective

To develop the ability to attack in behind a deep defensive line - quality and timing of run and final pass.

Description 9 v 9

Using half a full size pitch, we have 1 central zone (65 yards x 30 yards) and 2 end zones (65 yards x 18 yards and 65 yards x 8 yards). There are 2 normal full size goals at each end. The smallest zone is a safe zone for the white team when they have possession (the red team cannot enter). The white team are in a 2-2-3-1 formation and the red team are in a 4-4 formation.

The whites are looking to play the ball into the final zone for an attacking player (teammate) to run onto. The defenders are not allowed inside this zone before the ball is played in there. The red team are free to score from anywhere if they win possession.

Different rules: 1) In the central zone, the red defenders can intercept the ball, but are unable to tackle opponents. **2)** No defenders are allowed in the final zone and the attacker has a maximum 2 touches to score. **3)** 1 defender and 2 attackers allowed in the final zone at a time. **4)** The team in possession are limited to 2 touches and can only score with a 1 touch finish. **5)** There has to be 1 less defender in the final zone than attackers and the attackers are limited to 2 touches (still have to finish with 1 touch).

GOAL ANALYSIS
Timing Runs in Behind to be Onside

14-Apr-12
Real Madrid 3-1 Sporting Gijon (3rd Goal): Benzema - Assist: Ozil

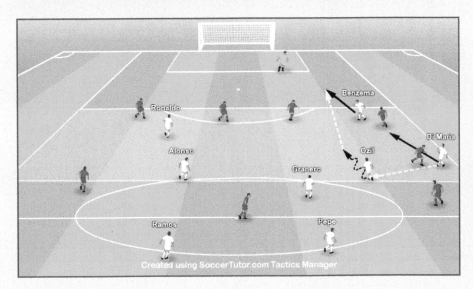

Di Maria recognises the numerical advantage in the centre of the field and passes to Ozil. Ozil dribbles forward and exploits the poor positioning of the left back and passes with good timing to Benzema.

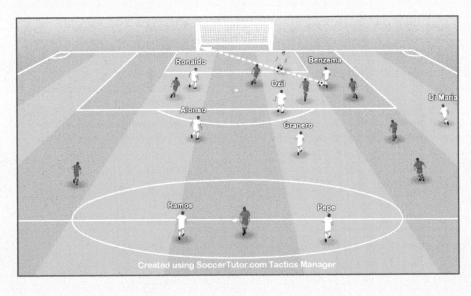

Benzema takes a good first touch towards the goal and finishes in the far corner.

SESSION FOR THIS TOPIC *(4 Practices)*

1. Attacking Combinations & Finishing with the Offside Rule

Objective

To develop quick combination play in and around the penalty area with the offside rule.

Description

In this functional practice, we have an area double the size of the penalty area split into 2 zones. The 4 white attacking players (from the 4-2-3-1) play against 4 defenders. We also have 2 neutral players outside at the end without the goal (one each side). The 2 neutral players act as the 2 central midfielders in the 4-2-3-1.

The white team use quick combinations to work a position inside the box and score a goal past the goalkeeper. If the defenders win the ball, their aim is to keep possession for as long as possible using the 2 neutral players.

Rules:

1. Limit the players to 1 or 2 touches.
2. Apply the offside rule.

Coaching Points

1. Good decision making, creativity and quick transitions are needed from the white team.
2. The collaboration of the run and the pass is again key, as well as making sure to coordinate the runs in behind to attack different areas of space (which stretches the defenders and causes imbalance).
3. This practice should be played at a high tempo with quick forward passing and movement to create space.

PROGRESSION

2. 6v5 (+GK) Attacking and Finishing with the Offside Rule (1)

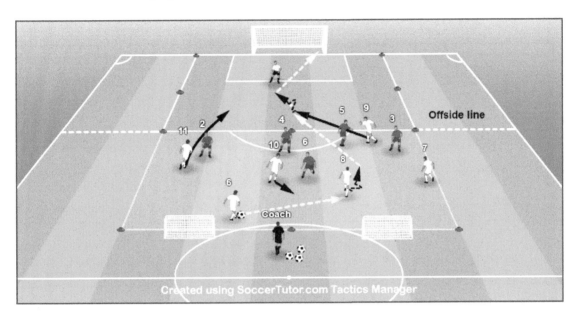

Description

Now the white team have 2 central midfielders and the blue team has 1 central midfielder. The objective for the white team is the same and the blues now aim to score in the 2 mini goals if they win the ball.

Rules:

1. Limit the players to 1-2 touches.
2. Apply the offside rule.

VARIATION

3. 6v5 (+GK) Attacking and Finishing with the Offside Rule (2)

Description

The variation is that the blue team's formation has changed to a 2-2-1. The full backs have been removed, and they now have 2 centre backs, 2 central midfielders and 1 attacking midfielder.

Rules:

1. Limit the players to 1-2 touches.
2. Apply the offside rule.

PROGRESSION

4. Attacking and Finishing with the Offside Rule in a SSG

Description

We now have a full size goal at both ends.

You can also use this progression for the blue team's formation variation in the previous practice on the last page.

Rules:

1. Limit the players to 1 or 2 touches.

2. Apply the offside rule.

CHAPTER 2

ATTACKING AGAINST OPPONENTS WHO USE A MIDDLE DEFENSIVE LINE

Goal Analysis: Creating Space for 1v1 Situations on the Flank 88
SESSION FOR THIS TOPIC *(5 Practices)*
1. Creating Space on the Flank and Timing Runs from the Centre in an Unopposed Practice 91
2. Creating Space on the Flank and Timing Runs from the Centre in an Opposed Practice 92
3. 2v2 on the Flanks with Crossing and Finishing... 93
4. 2v2 on the Flanks with Support from the Centre.. 93
5. Creating a 1v1 Situation on the Flank 94

Goal Analysis: Midfield Forward Runs in Behind the Defence 95
SESSION FOR THIS TOPIC *(4 Practices)*
1. Forward Runs and Through Balls in a Zonal Game... 98
2. Timing Runs in Between Defenders in a 4 Zone Game... 99
3. Timing Runs in Between Defenders in a 9v9 Game...100
4. Timing Runs in a Position Specific Zonal Practice..101

Goal Analysis: Through Balls from the Flank into the Centre & in Behind 102
SESSION FOR THIS TOPIC *(4 Practices)*
1. 6v6 (+2) 'End Zone' Final Ball Game..105
2. Diagonal Through Balls from Wide Areas (1) 106
3. Diagonal Through Balls from Wide Areas (2) 107
4. Passing in Behind a Middle Defensive Line in a 9v9 Game 107

Goal Analysis: Long Switch of Play to Create Space for a Final Ball..108
PRACTICE FOR THIS TOPIC
1. Switching Play and Through Balls Against a Middle Defensive Line in a 5 Zone Position Specific Practice.........109

ATTACKING AGAINST OPPONENTS WHO USE A MIDDLE DEFENSIVE LINE

When Real Madrid defended against an opposition which used a middle defensive line, they wanted to exploit the space in behind the defensive line. The objective was to retain safe possession of the ball and use combinations to work the ball into areas of the pitch where Real were strong and the opposition was weakest.

1. When the opposition's weakness was the lack of speed in the full back position, Real Madrid would aim to get the ball into wide areas to their wide forwards (especially Ronaldo). They looked to create 1v1 situations on the flank and exploit the space in behind the full back. The other players would use their speed to get into good positions inside the penalty area to finish a pass or cross from out wide (if the wide forward did not shoot himself).

2. When the opposition had good defensive organisation with the correct distances and strong full backs, Real would look to maintain safe possession and work the ball from one side of the pitch to the other. In the situations when one of Real's wide players had possession, a central player would make a diagonal cutting run in between the full back and centre back to create a numerical advantage on the flank (2v1).

3. When an opposition used a middle defensive line and had slower/weaker players in the centre, Jose Mourinho's team would look to keep patient possession until the time was right to play a through ball in between the defenders. Madrid could exploit the space very well with the speed of their attacking players to get in behind the central defenders and score.

GOAL ANALYSIS
Creating Space for 1v1 Situations on the Flank (1)

15-Oct-11
Real Madrid 4-1 Real Betis (1st Goal): Higuain - Assist: Ronaldo

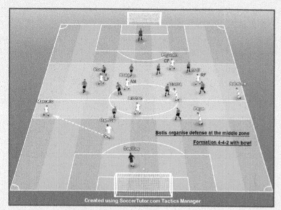

The opposition play with a middle defensive line and have a high concentration of players in the centre of the pitch. Marcelo and Arbeloa occupy the wide positions, as Ozil and Ronaldo take up positions on the inside. Ramos starts the attack from the back with a pass to the left back (Marcelo).

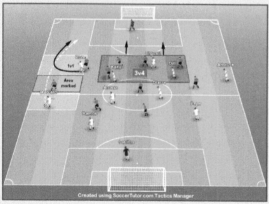

Marcelo's direct opponent moves up to close him down but is unable to prevent the pass. Ronaldo makes a curved run from his position to receive the pass down the line from Marcelo. He is now in space and is in a 1v1 situation with the opposition right back.

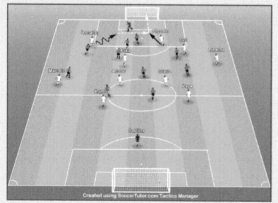

Ronaldo is too quick and too skilful for the defender and takes advantage. He beats the man and dribbles the ball into the penalty area. He plays a low cross for Higuain who has made a run into the box and finishes with 1 touch.

GOAL ANALYSIS
Creating Space for 1v1 Situations on the Flank (2)

26-Nov-11

Real Madrid 4-1 Atletico Madrid (2ⁿᵈ Goal): Di Maria - Assist: Ronaldo

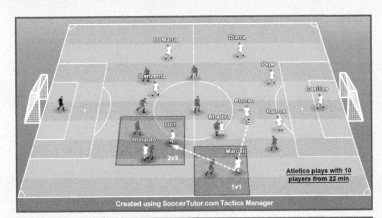

Alonso passes to Marcelo on the left and he is closed down. Ozil supports him in a position behind the back of the midfield line. Marcelo makes the pass which eliminates the 4 midfielders from the game.

Ronaldo has taken up a good position between the right back and the central defender. Ozil plays the pass ahead of Ronaldo into the space utilising his speed and quality in 1v1 situations.

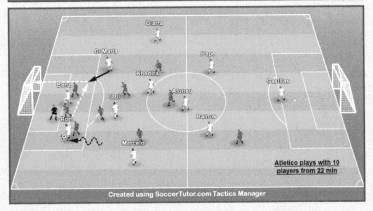

Ronaldo is too quick again and dribbles the ball into the penalty area where the defenders close him down. He again hits a low cross, to Di Maria this time who arrives at the back post from the opposite flank and finishes with 1 touch.

GOAL ANALYSIS
Creating Space for 1v1 Situations on the Flank (3)

04-Mar-12

Real Madrid 5-0 Espanyol (3rd Goal): Higuain- Assist: Kaka

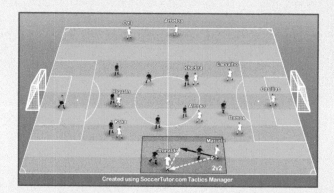

The ball is with the left back Marcelo again. He is supported by Ronaldo and we have 2v2 situation on the side. Marcelo plays a quick one-two combination with Ronaldo and breaks through the opponent's pressing.

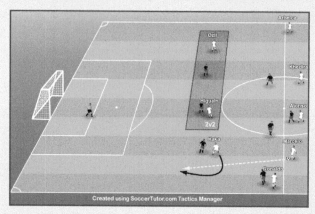

Marcelo plays a first time pass to Kaka who allows the ball to run and attacks the space in behind the full back in another successful 1v1 situation for Real Madrid on the flank.

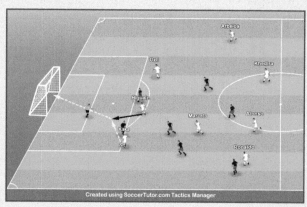

Kaka dribbles the ball up to the edge of the penalty area where the opposition's central defender moves towards him. Higuain sees this and makes a diagonal run into the space behind him. Kaka passes into this space at the correct time and Higuain scores.

SESSION FOR THIS TOPIC *(5 Practices)*

1. Creating Space on the Flank and Timing Runs from the Centre in an Unopposed Practice

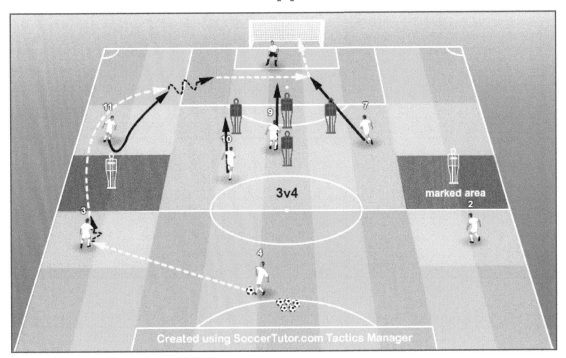

Objective

To develop attacking play on the flank - exploiting 1v1 situations by utilising the wide forwards.

Description

Using three quarters of a pitch, we create 3 zones on each side and 1 zone in the centre. In the middle side zones we have 1 mannequin and we have 4 mannequins in the central zone. We have 1 central defender or central midfielder, 2 full backs, 2 wide forwards, 1 attacking midfielder and 1 striker.

The drill starts with the CD/CM who passes to either the left back (3) or right back (2). They use 2 touches to first receive and then pass into space for the wide forward. The wide forward makes a checked movement (as if away from a marker) and changes direction using explosive speed to sprint and drive the ball towards the penalty area. He then hits a low cross/pass to oncoming players in the centre.

Coaching Points

1. This practice needs a variety of different passes - to feet, into space, short, long, curved etc and all need to be accurate and weighted correctly for the combination play to flow.

2. Players should check away before moving to receive the ball.

3. We should develop quality crossing, 1 touch finishing and coordination of movement to the final ball.

PROGRESSION

2. Creating Space on the Flank and Timing Runs from the Centre in an Opposed Practice

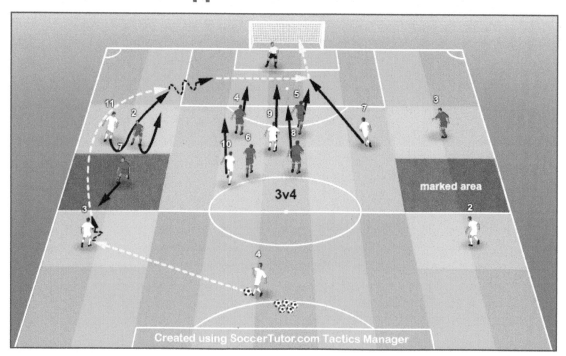

Description

In this progression we have introduced 7 active opponents to make this practice opposed.

The right midfielder (7) and the left midfielder (8) of the opponent have to be ready to move from the central zone when the first pass is played and press the full back. Once they are in the 'marked area' they are not allowed to leave it. The white full back is not allowed to enter the 'marked area.'

In the side zones nearest the penalty area, only the red team's full backs and the white team's wide forwards can enter (1v1 situation). In the central zone we have a 3v4 situation and all players here (attackers and defenders) can enter the box to try and score from or defend the cross. The full back on the opposite side is not allowed in the box.

Coaching Points

1. Good timing of movement/passing and communication needed in the side zones.

2. Players need to check away from their marker before moving to receive the ball (especially the wide forwards in the 1v1 situation).

3. The players making runs into the box need to coordinate so they move into different areas (near post, far post etc).

PROGRESSION

3. 2v2 on the Flanks with Crossing and Finishing

Description

In this progression we encourage combination play between the full back and the wide forward. The full backs can go in the 'marked area' (middle zone). They are still not allowed in the zone closest to the penalty area.

PROGRESSION

4. 2v2 on the Flanks with Support from the Centre

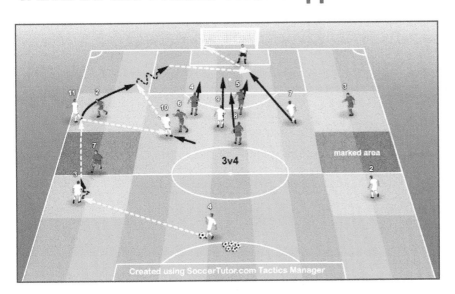

Description

The one difference in this progression is that the wide forwards are now allowed to pass and combine with the attacking midfielder in the central zone. However, neither player is allowed to leave their respective zone.

PROGRESSION

5. Creating a 1v1 Situation on the Flank

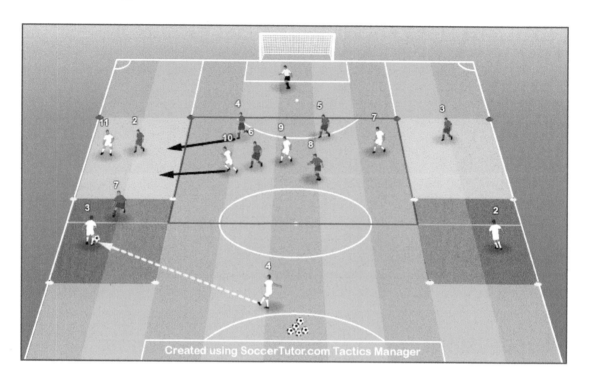

Created using SoccerTutor.com Tactics Manager

Description

This progression allows 1 player from the central zone (attacking midfielder or striker) to enter the side zone and combine with the full back and wide forward. One member of the red team (defensive team) can follow the player into the side zone.

The objective remains the same, which is to work a scenario where the wide forward gets into in a 1v1 situation on the flank against the opposition's full back. He can then put a low cross into the penalty area for the other attacking players to score.

GOAL ANALYSIS
Midfield Forward Runs in Behind the Defence (1)

28-Aug-11
Zaragoza 0-6 Real Madrid (5ᵗʰ Goal): Kaka

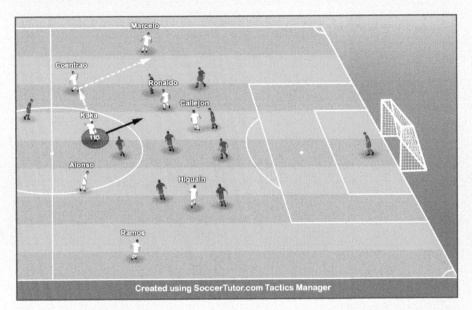

Zaragoza are organised and have many players in the centre of the pitch. Kaka passes to Coentrao and he passes to Marcelo on the left flank. Real are utilizing the full width of the pitch, but the defence is organised and they have many players behind the ball.

Kaka supports Marcelo and makes a diagonal run in between the centre back and the right back. Marcelo passes into the space behind the defensive line for Kaka to run onto.

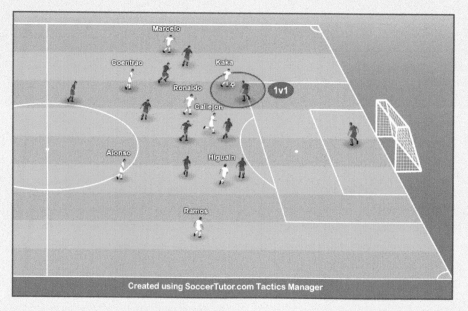

Kaka receives the ball and now has a 1v1 situation against the centre back. His teammates leave the space free for Kaka to exploit.

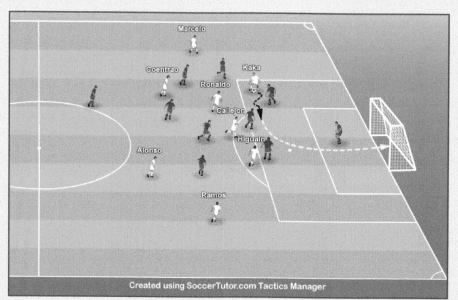

Kaka shows good ability and movement by cutting inside onto his right foot and shooting into the far corner of the net.

GOAL ANALYSIS
Midfield Forward Runs in Behind the Defence (2)

02-Oct-11
Espanyol 0-4 Real Madrid (2ⁿᵈ Goal): Higuain - Assist: Arbeloa

Diarra passes to Arbeloa. Ozil makes a movement to support him. The left back follows Ozil and leaves free space in behind. Higuain is alert to the situation and makes a diagonal run into the free space.

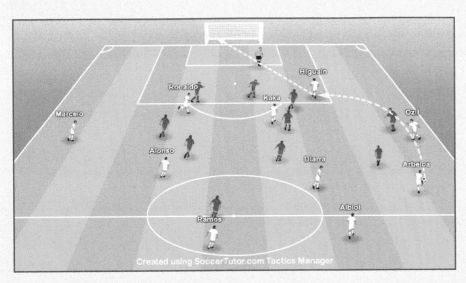

Arbeloa plays a lofted pass into the space for Higuain who produces a great first time finish into the far corner.

SESSION FOR THIS TOPIC *(4 Practices)*
1. Forward Runs and Through Balls in a Zonal Game

Created using SoccerTutor.com Tactics Manager

Objective

Develops attacking combinations to create chances in behind the defensive line. Practicing the final pass and diagonal runs in between the full back and centre back when the opposition hold a middle defensive line.

Description 7 v 7 (+2 Neutral Players)

We use an area 60 yards x 45 yards. In the centre we have 3 zones. The middle zone is 30 yards x 30 yards and the 2 side zones are 7.5 yards x 30 yards. We also have 2 final zones with goalkeepers, which are 15 yards x 30 yards each. We play 6v6 in the centre with both teams using a 2-3-1 formation .

The team in possession has 2 Neutral players at the sides to play with (who must stay in their zone). The defenders cannot enter the final zone until the ball is played in there.

Different rules: 1) No defenders allowed in the side zones. **2)** 1 defender is allowed in the side zone at a time and is fully active. **3)** Unlimited entry into the side zones.

PROGRESSION

2. Timing Runs in Between Defenders in a 4 Zone Game

Created using SoccerTutor.com Tactics Manager

Description 8 v 6 +GK

15 yards past the halfway line we place 2 mini goals. We have 3 zones; 1 central which is 44 yards x 44 yards and 2 side zones which are 40 yards x 20 yards. There is a 6v6 situation in the central zone with the white team in a 2-3-1 formation and the red team in a 4-2 formation. The white team also have 2 additional players (full backs) who only play in their respective side zones. All players in the red team can move into any of the zones.

The white team's objective is to exploit the numerical advantage at the sides, making diagonal runs in between the opposition full back and centre back to support their full back in possession.

The aim is to get into the final zone and score. The red team aim to win the ball and have a maximum of 5-6 passes or 10-15 seconds to score in 1 of the 2 mini goals.

Different rules

1. Unlimited touches in the centre and the full back has 2 touches.

2. Limit players to 3 touches in the centre and the full back has 2 touches.

3. Maximum of 2 touches in the final zone.

4. Players limited to 2 touches in the final zone but only 1 touch to finish.

5. All touches in the final zone limited to 1.

PROGRESSION

3. Timing Runs in Between Defenders in a 9v9 Game

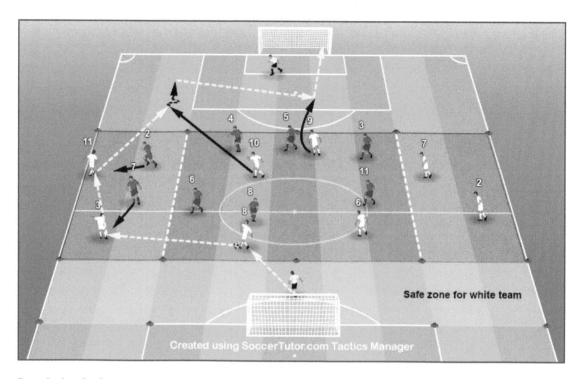

Safe zone for white team

Created using SoccerTutor.com Tactics Manager

Description 9 v 9

In this progression we have the same objective, but we have added an extra zone with a goalkeeper (safe zone for white team) which runs the full width of the pitch and up to the edge of the penalty area. The white team are using a 2-2-3-1 formation and the other team a 4-4 formation.

The white team now have a safe zone near their own goal which the red team are not allowed to enter. If the white take switches the play from one side zone to the other they get 1 point, if they complete 8 consecutive passes they get 2 points and if they score a goal they get 3 points.

From the white team, 6, 8, 10, 11 and 7 can move freely across all zones (2 and 3 must remain only in the side zones). From the red team, only 2, 7, 3 and 11 can enter the side zones. The defenders are not allowed to enter the final zone before the ball is played in there. When the ball goes out, we always start again with the goalkeeper.

Different rules

1. Unlimited touches in the centre and 2 touches in the final zone.

2. 3 touches in the centre and 2 touches in the final zone.

3. Some key players allowed unlimited touches and the others have limited touches.

4. All the previous options with the players limited to 1 touch finishing.

PROGRESSION

4. Timing Runs in a Position Specific Zonal Practice

Created using SoccerTutor.com Tactics Manager

Description 11 vs 11

From the previous practice, we now use a full pitch and add 2 central defenders for the white team and 2 attackers for the red team.

When the white team has possession in the low zone, the only red players that are allowed in there are 9 and 10. Once the ball is played into the middle zone, the other 8 red players press the ball and defend. White 4 & 5 and red 9 & 10 are not allowed in the middle once the ball is played in there. If the reds win the ball in the middle zone, all players are allowed to attack/defend in the red's high zone (white team's low zone).

The red team should have a maximum amount of touches or time to finish their attack if they win the ball.

Rules for the white players

1. Unlimited touches in the centre and 2 touches in the final zone
2. In the centre limit the touches and 2 touches in the final zone.
3. Some key players have unlimited touches, while the others have limited touches.
4. With all the previous options limit the finishing to 1 touch.
5. All players in the final zone limited to 1 touch.

GOAL ANALYSIS
Through Balls from the Flank into the Centre & in Behind (1)

02-Oct-11

Espanyol 0-4 Real Madrid (4ᵗʰ Goal): Higuain - Assist: Marcelo

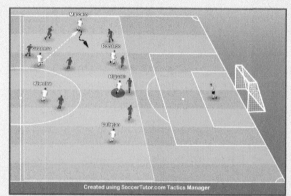

Granero passes to Marcelo on the left, who dribbles inside.

Marcelo plays a pass in behind the defensive line between the 2 central defenders and into the free space. Higuain has made a run behind the back of the other central defender.

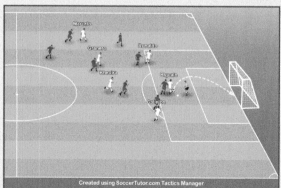

Higuain receives the though pass in space and with a very good 1 touch finish scores a goal.

GOAL ANALYSIS
Through Balls from the Flank into the Centre & in Behind (2)

15-Oct-11

Real Madrid 4-1 Real Betis (3rd Goal): Higuain - Assist: Di Maria

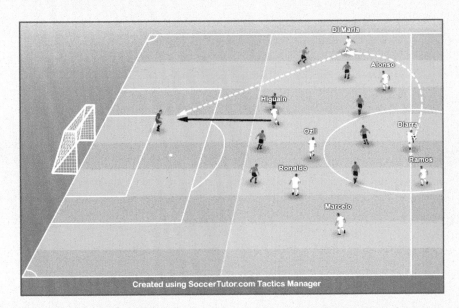

Diarra passes to Di Maria on the right side and faces a well organised defence to his left and in front of him. Higuain recognises the situation and makes a run in between the 2 centre backs. Di Maria displays excellent vision and decision making by playing a ball in behind the back 4 which neutralises 8 players.

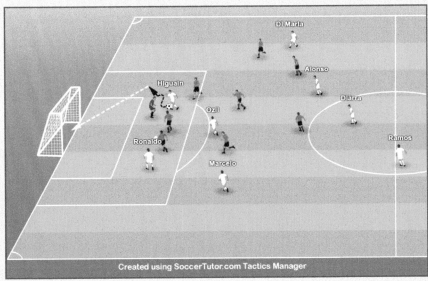

Higuain times his run perfectly into the free space and takes a good first touch, dribbles the ball round the goalkeeper and scores in the open net.

GOAL ANALYSIS
Through Balls from the Flank into the Centre & in Behind (3)

28-Jan-12
Real Madrid 3-1 Zaragoza (1st Goal): Kaka - Assist: Carvalho

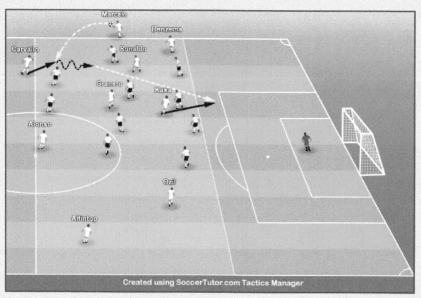

Created using SoccerTutor.com Tactics Manager

Marcelo throws to Carvalho. The opposition have 10 players close to the ball in that half of the pitch (with the midfield and defensive lines very close to each other). Carvalho dribbles forwards and with 1 pass in between the right back and centre back, finds Kaka in behind the defensive line (taking 10 opposition players out of the game)

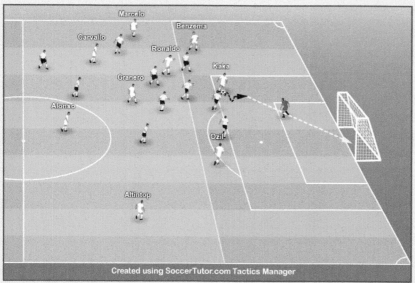

Created using SoccerTutor.com Tactics Manager

Kaka has a good first touch and nice finish to score a goal.

SESSION FOR THIS TOPIC *(4 Practices)*
1. 6v6 (+2) 'End Zone' Final Ball Game

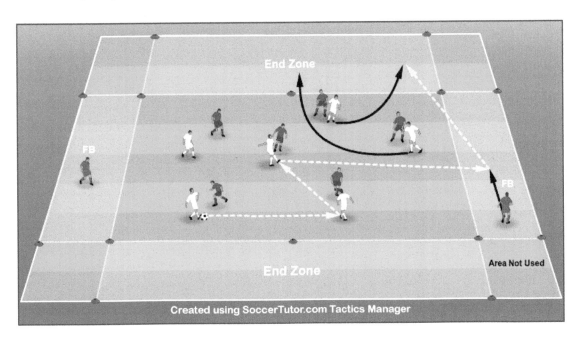

Objective

Develops attacking combinations to create chances in behind when the opposition hold a middle defensive line.

Description 6 v 6 (+2 Neutral Players)

In an area 60 yards x 45 yards, we have 5 zones. In the centre we have 3 zones, 1 middle zone (30 yards x 30 yards) and 2 side zones (7.5 yards x 30 yards). We also have 2 end zones (15 yards x 30 yards each). We play 6v6 with both using a 2-3-1 formation, with the aim to receive the ball in the 'End Zone.' The team in possession plays with the 2 neutral players at the side who can only move in this area. The defenders are not allowed to enter the end zones before the ball is played in there.

Different rules: 1) No defenders allowed in the side zones. **2)** The defenders are fully active, but only 1 can enter the side zones at a time. **3)** Unlimited touches and neutral players with 2 touches/ 1-2 touches and neutral players with 2 touches. **4)** Add a 3rd neutral player to play in the central zone. **5)** All players (including neutral) in the central zone have 1 touch and the side neutral players have 2 touches.

Coaching Points

1. Players should be aiming to change the direction of play and pass to the neutral players on the side, exploiting their numerical advantage and extra width.
2. The inside players should be making runs to receive the ball in the end zones from the neutral players and communication with their teammates to make opposite runs (as shown in the diagram) to create space for each other.
3. The timing of the run and the pass needs to be well coordinated.

PROGRESSION

2. Diagonal Through Balls from Wide Areas (1)

Description 8 v 8+GK (+3 Neutral Players)

15 yards beyond the halfway line we place 4 mini goals. The playing area is split into 2 zones; we make a line of cones 10 yards from the penalty area. The largest zone is 40 yards x 65 yards.

The white team use a 2-2-3-1 formation and when in possession they have help from 3 neutral players (2 at the sides and 1 in the centre). The neutrals players only take part when the white team is in possession. The blue team use a 4-4 formation.

The white team start the attack and must use quick combinations to get the ball into the final zone and in behind the defensive line. The blue defenders are not allowed to enter the end zones before the ball is played in there. If the blue team wins the ball, they try to score in the 4 mini goals and their goals count double.

Rules in the Central Zone:

1. All white players have unlimited touches and the neutral players have 2 / All players have 2-3 touches.
2. All white players and the central neutral player have 2-3 touches and the side neutral players have 1 touch.
3. White defenders, the striker and the neutral players have 2 touches, and the white AM, LF & RF are unlimited.
4. In the final zone progress from 3 to 2 to 1 touch for the key players.

PROGRESSION

3. Diagonal Through Balls from Wide Areas (2)

Description

8 v 8+GK
(+2 Neutral Players)

In this progression we have the same objective, but now we have just 2 neutral players and they are both inside the main zone. They play with the white team in possession only.

PROGRESSION

4. Passing in Behind a Middle Defensive Line in a 9v9 Game

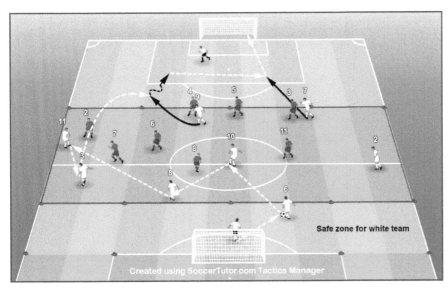

9 v 9

We remove the 4 mini goals and create a safe zone up to the edge of the box. We now have a full size goal at both ends. The red team start defending when the ball comes into the central zone (they are not allowed in the safe zone). If the reds win the ball, they have 10 seconds to score (quick transition).

GOAL ANALYSIS
Long Switch of Play to Create Space for a Final Ball

29-Oct-11

Real Sociedad 0-1 Real Madrid: Hguain - Assist: Coentrao

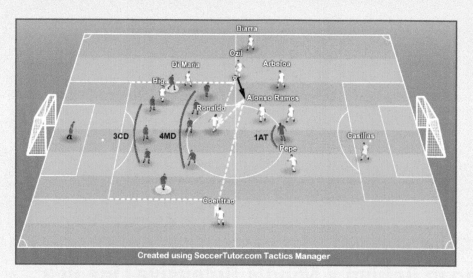

Real Sociedad played with a ball oriented defence using the 5-4-1, which made them very compact in closed lines in front of the box. Ozil plays a 1-2 with Ronaldo and then changes the direction of the play to the left with a long pass to Coentrao.

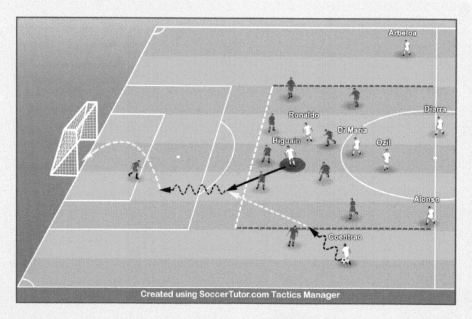

Coentrao is 1v1 against the right back. The centre back does not provide support and there is a large space between him and the right back created. Coentrao dribbles inside and Higuain makes a diagonal run into the space. The pass and run are timed perfectly and Real score.

PRACTICE FOR THIS TOPIC

1. Switching Play and Through Balls Against a Middle Defensive Line in a 5 Zone Position Specific Practice

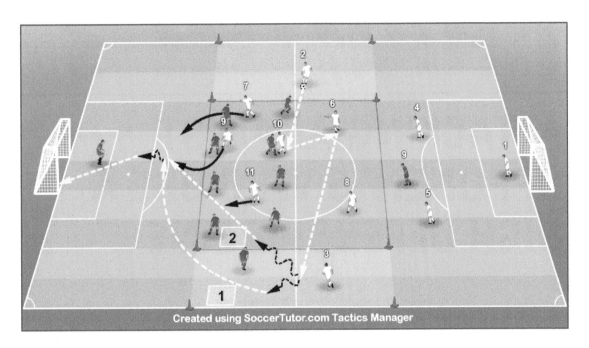

Created using SoccerTutor.com Tactics Manager

Objective

Develops attacking combinations to create chances in behind when the opposition hold a middle defensive line.

Description

We use a full pitch and create 3 zones in the middle third. The central zone is 40 yards x 40 yards.

The white team are in a 4-2-3-1 formation. The 2 central defenders (4 & 5) must stay outside the central zone, the 2 full backs (2 & 3) must stay in the side zones and the 2 central midfielders (6 & 8), the 2 wide forwards (7 and 11), the attacking midfielder (10) and the striker (9) play in the central zone unless the ball is played into the end zone by the full back.

The blue team are in a 5-4-1. They have 3 central defenders, 2 full backs and 4 midfield players. Only their full backs are allowed in the side zones. The striker must stay outside the central zone with 4 & 5 of the whites.

The aim for the white team is to attack their opponent by keeping possession and work a position to pass the ball wide to their full backs so they have a 1v1 situation on the flank. From there, the full back looks to 1) Pass into the space behind the 3 centre backs with teammates making supporting runs or 2) Dribble inside to unbalance the defensive line and play a shorter pass in behind the defensive line.

CHAPTER 3

ATTACKING AGAINST OPPONENTS WHO USE A HIGH DEFENSIVE LINE

Goal Analysis: Playing the Ball in Behind a High Defensive Line 112
SESSION FOR THIS TOPIC *(4 Practices)*
1. 4 Zone Possession Game...114
2. Position Specific 7v7 (+1) Possession Game 115
3. Building Up Play Through the Lines in a Position Specific Practice..117
4. Playing in Behind a High Defensive Line in an 11v11 Game...119

Goal Analysis: Building Up Play against Opponent's who Press High 120
SESSION FOR THIS TOPIC *(5 Practices)*
1. Breaking Through Pressure Possession Game...121
2. Dynamic Transitional Possession Game in the 4-2-3-1 122
3. Playing Through the Lines in a 3 Zone Small Sided Game...123
4. Breaking Through Pressure High Up the Pitch in a 3 Zone Game (1)...124
5. Breaking Through Pressure High Up the Pitch in a 3 Zone Game (2)...125

ATTACKING AGAINST OPPONENTS WHO USE A HIGH DEFENSIVE LINE

Some teams decide to defend against Real Madrid with a high line at the start of a match or sometimes during a match if they were behind and needed a goal or because a player had been sent off (11v10).

In these cases Real Madrid focused a lot of their game on getting round the back of their opponents. This was mainly with direct forward passes in behind the back four (especially in the lateral space in between the full back and the central defender).

Passes into space gave a big advantage to the quick Real players who had good dribbling ability and it also enabled the other players to quickly move up from the back to provide support and finish the attack.

In this phase with pressure from the opposition high up the pitch and a numerical disadvantage Real Madrid's objective would be:

1. Maintain possession with accurate passing to feet in the low zone.

2. Use 1 touch passing combined with quick support play (1-2 combinations) to break through the pressure.

3. Forward pass to the player highest up the pitch into space and in behind the high defensive line.

4. Provide fast support for this player to quickly finish the attack.

GOAL ANALYSIS
Playing the Ball in Behind a High Defensive Line (1)

24-Mar-12

Real Madrid 5-1 Real Sociedad (5th Goal): Ronaldo - Assist: Higuain

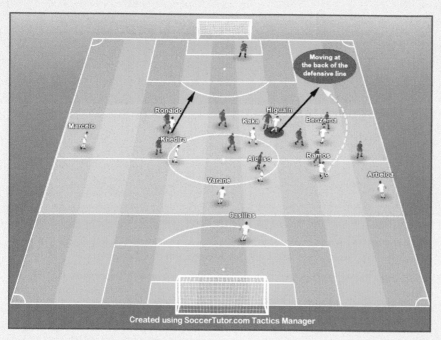

The opposition are very compact in closed lines high up the pitch. There is free space in behind the back 4. Ramos has the ball with 10 opponents in front of him, but with one pass round the back of the left back he neutralises all 10 players. Higuain leaves his direct opponent to make his diagonal run in behind. Ronaldo also starts to move and takes up a good position in the penalty area.

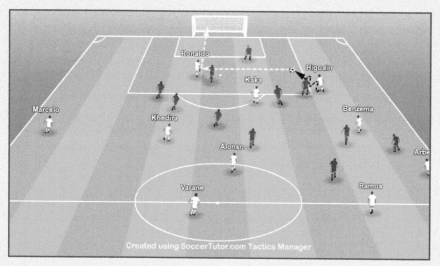

Higuain drives the ball across the box at the perfect time and the short parallel pass meets Ronaldo's movement into space and he scores.

GOAL ANALYSIS
Playing the Ball in Behind a High Defensive Line (2)

24-Sep-11
Real Madrid 6-2 Rayo Vallecano (6th Goal): Ronaldo - Assist: Ozil

The opposition are playing a very high line and Ramos with 1 pass inside to Ozil takes 6 players out of the game and gives the advantage to Real Madrid in the centre.

Ozil dribbles the ball further inside and Ronaldo makes a good diagonal run in between the right back and the central defender. The run and pass are timed perfectly for Ronaldo to receive in behind. Ronaldo takes the ball round the goalkeeper who brings him down for a penalty. He converts it himself to score.

SESSION FOR THIS TOPIC *(4 Practices)*
1. 4 Zone Possession Game

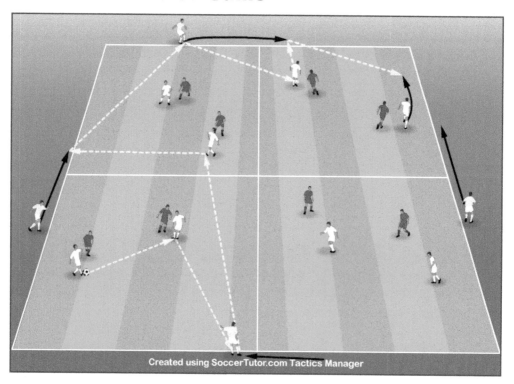

Created using SoccerTutor.com Tactics Manager

Objective

To develop possession play with high pressure in limited space and time.

Description 8 v 8 (+4 Neutral Players)

In an area 20 yards x 20 yards, we split the pitch into 4 grids which are 10 yards x 10 yards each. In each grid we have a 2v2 situation. We also have 4 neutral players who can move all the way along their side of the square without entering the grids. The neutral players play with the team in possession.

If a team completes 8 passes or keeps the ball for 10 seconds they win 1 point. If a team passes through all the grids without losing possession they get 2 points.

Different Rules: 1) Unlimited touches for regular players and neutral players are limited to 1 or 2 touches. **2)** 1 or 2 touches for all players.

Coaching Points

1. Correct body shape (open up on the half turn) and positioning is important to view where the options for where the next pass is going.

2. Players need to protect the ball in these 1v1/2v2 situations; put their body in between the opponent and the ball.

3. Key aspects: Speed and quality of pass, good decision making, correct angles and distances for support play and creative combination play and movement.

PROGRESSION

2. Position Specific 7v7 (+1) Possession Game

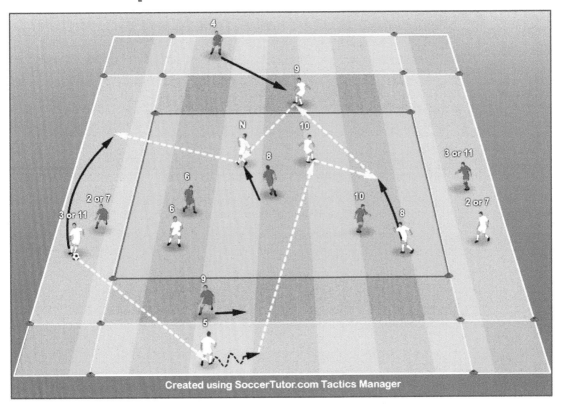

Created using SoccerTutor.com Tactics Manager

Objective

To develop possession play with high pressure in limited space and time.

Description 7 v 7 (+1 Neutral Player)

In an area 20 yards x 25 yards, we have 7 grids. In the central zone, we have 1 large grid which is 12 yards x 12 yards and 2 smaller grids which are both 2 yards x 12 yards. We have 4 grids on the outside which are 16 yards x 5 yards.

In the large central zone, we have 3v3 (+1 neutral player). In the side zones, we have wide players (full backs & wideforwards) in 1v1 situations. In the end zones we have a central defender (red 4 and white 5) and in front of them we have the striker (9). The central defender can enter the striker's zone, but the striker cannot enter his. The striker can only press the central defender from his zone with the objective of preventing/intercepting a pass.

If a team completes 6 passes or keeps possession for 8 seconds they get 1 point. If a team passes the ball through all the grids without losing possession they get 2 points.

Rules

1. The central defenders and the side players have 2-3 touches, strikers and the neutral have 1 touch, inside players with unlimited touches.

2. The central defenders and the side players have 2 touches, strikers and the neutral have 1 touch, inside players with 2-3 touches.

Coaching Points

1. The inside players need to be constantly thinking of changing the direction of play to the outside zones.

2. The side players (especially) need to check away from their markers before moving to receive the ball as they have limited space to play in.

3. Judging whether to play a pass to feet or into space for your teammate is important in this practice.

4. The side players need to be strong in their 1v1 situations (shield the ball from the opponent).

5. The angles, distances and quick/sharp movements of the support players is key to success in this practice.

PROGRESSION

3. Building Up Play Through the Lines in a Position Specific Practice

Objective

To develop possession play with high pressure in limited space and time (with support play).

Description 11 v 10

In an area 45 yards x 35 yards, we have one team with 1 GK and 4 players in white (the defenders), 2 in blue (the centre midfielders) and 4 in yellow (the AM, LF, RF and striker) using the 4-2-3-1. The other team have 10 players who are all wearing red. The red team are applying pressure high up the pitch. The objective is to play the ball out from the back under pressure from the opposition with limited space and time.

The players look to work through the lines and back; the ball moves from the white to blue, and then back to white who supports. The ball is then passed from white to yellow and back to blue who supports and finally to yellow.

If the multi-colour team completes 6-8 passes or keep possession for 8-10 seconds they get 1 point. If the ball is played from the GK, to white, to blue, to yellow and all the way back to the GK they get 2 points.

If the reds win possession, they must score within 5-6 passes in the goal. This is a quick transition for the multi-colour team from attack to defence.

Different Rules:

1. Whites have 2-3 touches, blues have 1 touch and yellows have unlimited touches.

2. Whites have 2-3 touches, blues have unlimited touches, yellows have 2-3 touches.

3. All players have unlimited touches.

Coaching Points

1. Correct body shape (open up on the half turn) and positioning is important to view where the options for where the next pass is going.

2. Decision making is important; when to hold the ball, play a first time pass or dribble forwards.

3. Creating space and checking away before moving to receive will be essential to maintain possession and build up through the lines.

4. Vertical passes are very effective and allows play to move forwards much quicker as they take multiple defenders out of the game.

5. Using the full width by switching the play from one side to the other maximises the space and makes it easier to maintain possession.

6. The attacking team must be very alert to a potential transition from attack to defence and quickly pressure the ball carrier (getting bodies back behind the ball).

7. The angles, distances and quick/sharp movements of the support players is key to success in this practice.

PROGRESSION

4. Playing in Behind a High Defensive Line in an 11v11 Game

Safe zone for white team

Created using SoccerTutor.com Tactics Manager

Objective

To develop the ability to attack in behind the defensive line against opponents who use a high defensive line.

Description

Using a full pitch, we split the area into 3 zones as shown in the diagram. The central zone is the high line defensive zone for the red team. There is a safe zone for the white team and the third zone is the final attacking zone for the white team.

The practice always starts with the white team in possession who build up play from the back under high pressure from the red team. The objective is to keep possession under pressure and breakdown this pressure with passes in behind the defensive line. The red team are not allowed in the safe zone and they can only enter the attacking zone once the ball has been played in there. The red team has 8-10 seconds or a maximum of 6-8 passes to score if they win the ball (quick transition play). This rule makes the white team have a quick transition to defend.

Rules

White team must complete 6-8 passes before passing the ball into the final zone.

GOAL ANALYSIS
Building Up Play against Opponents who Press High

17-Dec-11
Sevilla 2-6 Real Madrid (4th Goal): Di Maria - Assist: Benzema

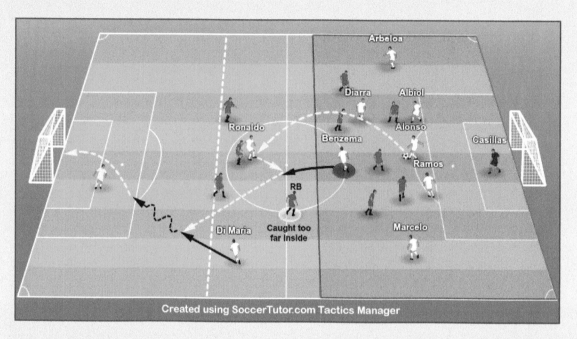

Created using SoccerTutor.com Tactics Manager

Sevilla press high up the pitch and Real want to break through the pressure. Alonso's direct pass to Ronaldo takes 6 players out of the game and because Sevilla pressed high up the pitch. Real have a numerical disadvantage (2v4) as they launch an attack. Benzema provides quick support to receive the pass back to him. from Ronaldo.

The Sevilla defensive line is caught out and the right back is in the wrong position. Benzema plays a first time pass to Di Maria into the space left by the right back on the left flank. Di Maria is faster than the central defender and with good dribbling speed drives into the box and scores the goal.

SESSION FOR THIS TOPIC *(5 Practices)*
1. Breaking Through Pressure Possession Game

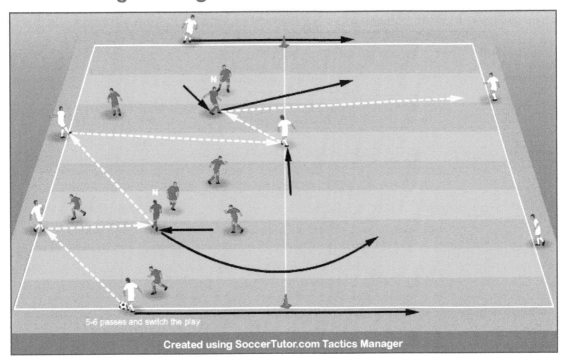

5-6 passes and switch the play

Created using SoccerTutor.com Tactics Manager

Objective

To develop possession play under intense pressure and changing the direction of attack; quick movements and support play.

Description 7 v 7 (+2 Neutral Players)

In an area 50 yards x 40 yards, we divide into 2 grids. We have 2 teams with 7 players each and 2 neutral players who play with the team in possession.

The drill starts in the left grid, 5 players have possession from one team with 2 neutral players against all 7 players of the opposition. The 5 players are in positions along the 4 sides of the grid; 2 at the back (centre backs), 1 left back and 1 right back (or wide forwards) and 1 on the middle line (AM or striker). The 2 neutral players move freely inside the grid to provide support (like central midfielders). The red team has a numerical advantage inside this grid. In the other half we have the 2 white players standing outside at the end.

The objective for the team in possession is to complete 5-6 passes and switch the play to the other side/grid. When this happens, the 2 wide players and the 2 neutral players move to support their teammates. All the opposition players also move across. The 2 at the back (centre backs) stay where they are, as does the player in the middle. The objective starts again with the play starting in the right grid. If the defending team wins the ball, the roles switch.

Variations:

1. When switching play from one grid to the other, the team must first keep possession for a minimum of 10 sec.

2. When there is a switch of play, the middle player changes with one of the bottom players who runs up quickly.

PROGRESSION

2. Dynamic Transitional Possession Game in the 4-2-3-1

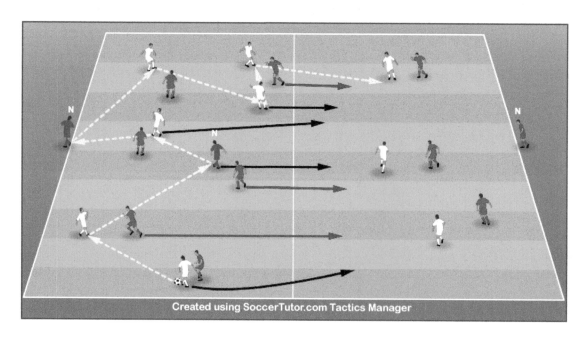

Created using SoccerTutor.com Tactics Manager

Objective

To develop possession play under intense pressure and changing the direction of attack; quick movements and support play.

Description 9 v 9 (+3 Neutral Players)

In an area 80 yards x 40 yards, we divide into 2 zones (40 yards x 40 yards each). The drill starts in the left grid with a 6v6 (+2 neutral players playing with the team in possession). The 6 white players can be in the 4-2 formation (part of the 4-2-3-1). The outside neutral player in the left grid has the role of goalkeeper. The inside neutral player is an extra man. On the other side the 3 players and 1 neutral can be the 3-1 part from the 4-2-3-1.

The objective is to keep possession of the ball under pressure in one grid and complete 6-8 passes. After this, the aim is to switch the play to the 3 players or neutral player in the other half. If this happens, 3 white players and the inside neutral player move across. 3 red players also move across, so we again have 6v6 (+2 neutral players playing with the team in possession). If the red team wins the ball they have the same objective. Either play with unlimited touches for normal players and limit the neutral's touches or limit all players touches.

Coaching Points

1. The players have to react quickly to the transition from attack to defence.

2. The pressure from the defenders should be well coordinated to make it as hard as possible for the other team to switch the play.

3. Key aspects: Speed and quality of pass, good decision making, correct angles and distances for support play and creative combination play and movement.

PROGRESSION

3. Playing Through the Lines in a 3 Zone Small Sided Game

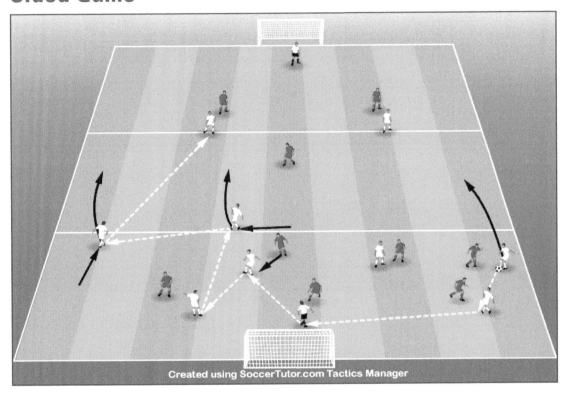

Created using SoccerTutor.com Tactics Manager

Description 9 v 9

Using the same size area of 80 yards x 40 yards, we divide the pitch into 3 zones this time. The 2 end zones are 36 yards x 40 yards each and the central zone is 12 yards x 40 yards. The drill starts in the 'low zone' grid with the goalkeeper + 7 players against 6. The team in possession uses a 4-2-1 formation with 1 player (AM) moving only parallel with the line and providing support.

In the 'middle zone', the red team has 1 player and the white team have 2 players who can only move along the line of the 3rd zone. In the final zone ('high zone'), the red team have 2 defenders and a goalkeeper. The objective is to maintain possession under pressure and complete 6-8 passes, then move the ball to one of the 2 players at the top who must play the ball back. If this happens, 3 white players move up and we have a 5v3 situation (should be quick passing and movement). The white team have 5-6 touches or 6-8 seconds to finish their attack.

If the defending team win the ball in the high or middle zones they try to score and the other team must make a quick transition to defend. If the defending team win the ball in the low zone they must keep possession and the teams change roles; the red team would then be set up exactly as the whites are shown in the diagram, but at the opposite end and the whites would be set up like the reds. If the ball goes out, the defending team start the drill from the opposite side and the teams change roles.

Different rules: 1) Unlimited touches in the low and middle zones and limited touches in the high zone. **2)** Unlimited touches in the low zone and limited touches in the middle and high zones. **3)** Limited touches in all of the zones.

PROGRESSION

4. Breaking Through Pressure High Up the Pitch in a 3 Zone Game (1)

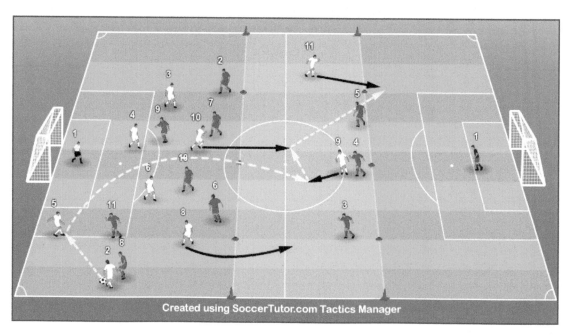

Created using SoccerTutor.com Tactics Manager

Description 10 v 11

We use a full pitch now. Divide into 3 zones (low , middle and high).The drill always starts in the low zone. The white team has 7 outfield players in the low zone (4-2-1) and the red team press high with 7 players. In the middle zone there are 2 white attackers v 3 red defenders.

The objective of the white team is to move a player from the low zone by playing a 1-2 with their teammate in the middle zone. This creates a 3v3 situation or 4v3 as one extra teammate is allowed to move up to the middle zone. This 4v3 should be exploited to create a chance and score.

Different rules:

1. Unlimited touches in the high and middle zones and limited touches in the low zone.

2. Unlimited touches in the high zone and limited touches in the middle and low zones.

3. Limited touches in all of the zones.

PROGRESSION

5. Breaking Through Pressure High Up the Pitch in a 3 Zone Game (2)

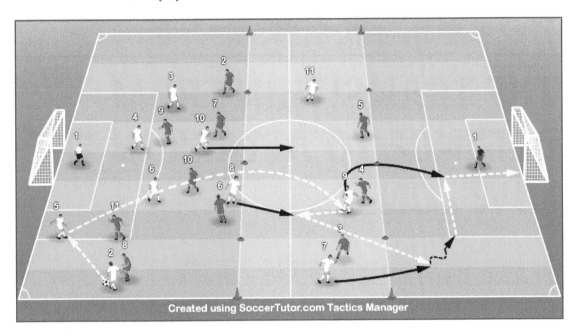

Created using SoccerTutor.com Tactics Manager

Description 11 v 11

Now we have 11v11 and we have 3v3 in the middle zone at the start of the drill. Now we can create a 5v3 situation for the attack.

CHAPTER 4

THE TRANSITION FROM DEFENCE TO ATTACK IN THE LOW ZONE

Goal Analysis: **Creating and Taking Advantage of 1v1 / 2v2 Situations** 130
SESSION FOR THIS TOPIC *(2 Practices)*
1. Unopposed Fast Break Attack Practice 132
2. Opposed Fast Break Attack with 1v1 / 2v2 Situations 133

Goal Analysis: **Quick Counter Attacking from the Low Zone** 134
SESSION FOR THIS TOPIC *(3 Practices)*
1. Transition & Support Play in a 3 Zone Dynamic Game 135
2. Transition & Support Play with Side Players 137
3. 11v11 Transition & Support Play in a 4 Zone Game 137

Goal Analysis: **Exploiting the Weak Side of the Opposition** 138
SESSION FOR THIS TOPIC *(5 Practices)*
1. 3 Team Counter Attacking Small Sided Game..140
2. Dynamic 3 Team Counter Attacking Small Sided Game...141
3. Playing Wide and Switching Play in a Transition Game 142
4. Exploiting the Weak Side of the Opponent in a 3 Zone Transition Game 143
5. Exploiting the Weak Side of the Opponent in a 3 Zone Transition Game using a Full Pitch 144

Goal Analysis: Long Pass to Switch Play to the Weak Side on the Break 145
SESSION FOR THIS TOPIC *(2 Practices)*
1. Fast Break and Switch of Play in a 5 Zone Game (1)...147
2. Fast Break and Switch of Play in a 5 Zone Game (2)...148

Goal Analysis: Creating and Exploiting Space on the Flanks 149
SESSION FOR THIS TOPIC *(5 Practices)*
1. Defensive Organisation to Win Possession with Quick Break from the Low Zone.........................151
2. Fast Combinations, Support and Finishing Practice 152
3. Fast Combinations, Support and Finishing Transition Game...153
4. Counter Attacking with a 4v3 Situation in a 3 Zone Game 154
5. Counter Attacking with a 4v4 Situation in a 3 Zone Game 155

Goal Analysis: Breaking from the Low Zone:
Causing Imbalance in a Defensive Line with a Delayed Pass...156
SESSION FOR THIS TOPIC *(2 Practices)*
1. Support Play in a Low Zone Transition Small Sided Game 158
2. Fast Break Attacks in Behind the Defensive Line in a Low Zone Transition Game 159

THE TRANSITION FROM DEFENCE TO ATTACK IN THE LOW ZONE

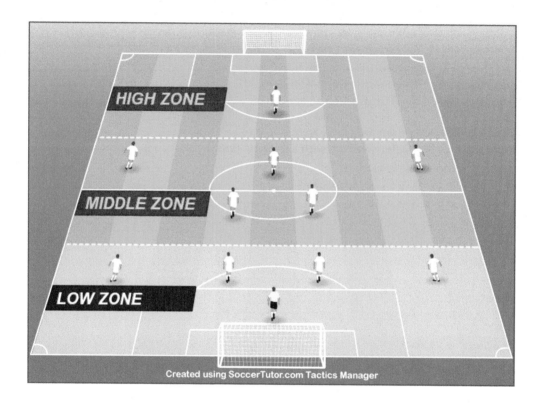

The main weapon for Real Madrid during the 2011-2012 season, like every other team Jose Mourinho has managed was the phase of the game in transition from defence to attack. In this phase Real were the best team in Europe. Depending on the particular opponent and how they defended and where they lost ball, Real Madrid would find the quickest and most effective solutions to enter the penalty area and score a goal.

Real Madrid played very intelligently in this phase, so whether they wanted to give space to an opponent with weak and slow transitions or because of the situation in the match, they would often have many players in the low zone and only 1 or 2 players near the halfway line. Their objective was to move into a transition from defence to attack very quickly using forward passes into space and exploiting their faster and higher quality players in 2v2 or 1v1 situations. In these cases, the time they took to finish their attack was between 9 and 12 seconds.

In many cases during the transition phases from the low zone, Real attacked with 4 players who would look to play the ball to one side at the correct time to fully exploit the space on the opposite side of the opponent (the weak side at that moment). In these cases, the breaks were faster than the previous ones and more entertaining with the attacks finishing in between 7 and 9 seconds.

In the third case when the opposition had lots of players in the centre, 1 or 2 Real players would quickly move up to provide support, very quickly coming from the back and the sides (usually the left or right forward) to call for the ball in the space in front. The wide forwards took up better positions than the defenders in this situation, using their speed to assist or score a goal. The average time to finish these attacks was about 10 seconds.

And in the last case we have the situation when the opposition lose possession in the low zone and Real Madrid would dribble up to the defensive line (causing imbalance) and use delayed passes in behind the defensive line. Usually in these cases the opposition had 4 or 5 players behind the ball, but not many quick players tracking back to support. So Real would enter a transition to attack in a 4v4 or 5v5 situation.

The objective was to dribble up to the penalty area and then pass to a teammate free in space who was normally on the flank. They would then use low crosses in between the last defenders and goalkeeper to score.

GOAL ANALYSIS
Creating and Taking Advantage of 1v1 / 2v2 Situations

02-Oct-11

Espanyol 0-4 Real Madrid (1ˢᵗ Goal): Higuain - Assist: Ronaldo

Real won the ball with Alonso in the low zone. Alonso passes to Kaka and the team make a quick transition to attack.

Kaka dribbles the ball and exploits the 1v1 situation because Higuain and Ronaldo do not give him good support.

Ronaldo reads the situation and makes a diagonal run cutting to the other side (free space behind the back of the centre back). Kaka passes the ball to him.

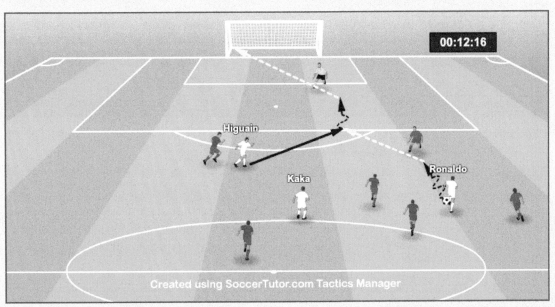

Ronaldo drives towards the box and Higuain comes from the left and provides good support in behind Ronaldo's direct opponent.

Ronaldo passes the ball to Higuain in behind who scores inside the box. From Alonso's 1st pass to the goal it took 12.16 seconds.

SESSION FOR THIS TOPIC *(2 Practices)*
1. Unopposed Fast Break Attack Practice

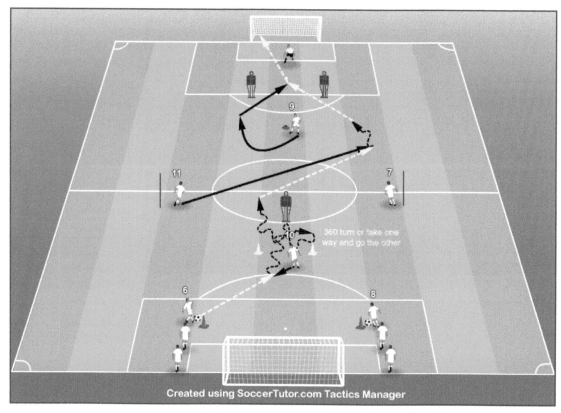

Created using SoccerTutor.com Tactics Manager

Objective

To develop fast break attacks and exploit 1v1 or 2v2 situations.

Description

Using a full pitch we have cones, mannequins and players as shown in the diagram above. The drill starts with player 6 inside the penalty area. He passes to player 10. He takes a quick directional first touch, turns and dribbles forward. Before he reaches the mannequin he must make a 360 degree turn or fake one way and go the other.

At this point, No.11 starts to make a diagonal opposite run to create space on the right side of the pitch. Player 10 passes to him in the space and No.11 receives and dribbles forward. Player 9 makes a checked/unmarking movement and calls for the ball in the space in behind the 2 mannequins (2 centre backs) AND between the 2 of them. 11 passes to him and 9 receives and shoots on goal. The drill then starts again from the other side.

Coaching Points

1. For the first pass No.10 should check away and then move to receive the pass to feet.
2. When dribbling in the centre, there needs to be close control with little touches, but it should be done at pace with a change of direction as if trying to beat a defender in a match.
3. In the attacking half, the key is the accuracy and correct weight of pass coordinated with the timing of the runs.

PROGRESSION

2. Opposed Fast Break Attack with 1v1 / 2v2 Situations

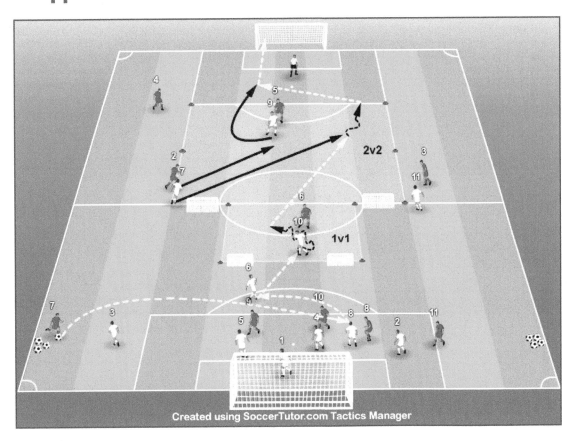

Created using SoccerTutor.com Tactics Manager

Description

Now we make the practice fully opposed with 11v11.

In the low zone we have balls on the left and right side. 7 and 11 from the red team cross the balls. As shown, when 7 crosses the ball, the white left back (3) presses him and inside the box we have a 4v4 situation. The objective for the white players is to defend the cross and clear the ball to the centre midfielder (6).

If this happens and Player 6 receives the ball, he passes to Player 10. Player 10 is in a 1v1 with the red centre midfielder (6) and his objective is to dribble past him. If the red player wins the ball he aims to score in a mini goal.

If Player 10 beats his man, he then passes into the next zone to 7 or 11 as one of them will make a diagonal run. 11 or 7 then play 2v2 with their striker against 2 red defenders. From the time the white Player 6 receives the ball, the team must finish their attack in a maximum of 12 seconds.

GOAL ANALYSIS
Quick Counter Attacking from the Low Zone

02-Oct-11

Espanyol 0-4 Real Madrid (3rd Goal): Callejon - Assist: Ronaldo

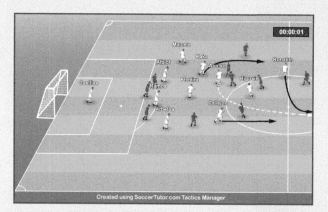

The opposition are caught very high up the pitch as they lose possession. Alonso again passes forwards into the free space in the other half of the pitch. This is into an area for Ronaldo to run onto (who is the furthest player forward at the time).

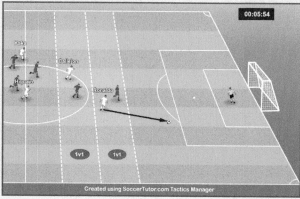

Ronaldo is quicker and better than his opponent in the 1v1. Callejon follows from behind being marked by 1 defender. We have 2 x 1v1 situations.

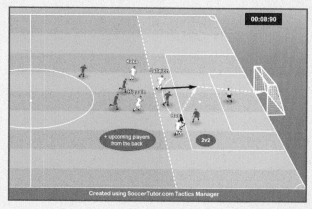

Ronaldo is too quick again and dribbles the ball into the penalty area where the defenders close him down. He again hits a low cross, to Di Maria this time who arrives at the back post from the opposite flank and finishes with 1 touch.

From the time Alonso passed the ball to the ball being in the net, this counter attack took 8.9 seconds.

SESSION FOR THIS TOPIC *(3 Practices)*

1. Transition & Support Play in a 3 Zone Dynamic Game

Created using SoccerTutor.com Tactics Manager

Objective

To develop transitions from defence to attack in the low zone and taking advantage of 1v1 or 2v2 situations.

Description

In an area 60 yards x 40 yards, we divide the pitch into 3 grids. The central zone is 10 yards x 40 yards and the 2 outside zones are 25 yards x 40 yards.

The practice starts in one outside zone with one team in possession like above in the diagram. We have 8 attackers (red) vs 6 defenders (white) and 1 neutral player (blue). The red team has 4 midfielders and 2 attackers inside this zone and 2 full backs who move only along the sides (2 & 3). The white team has 4 defenders and 2 central midielders (from the 4-2-3-1). The Blues (neutral) play with whoever is in possession. In the central zone we have a 1v1 situation and 2 side forwards for the white team who only move along the sides. In the other outside zone we have a 1v1 between white 9 and red 5.

In the first zone, the red team has the objective to keep possession and they get 1 point when they complete 6-8 passes. The aim for the white team is to steal the ball and pass quickly into the central zone to Player 10. One player is allowed to move into the central zone to provide quick support to him and receive a pass back. The same player will then look to do the same again in the final zone with the striker (9). The 2 side players (7 & 11) provide support in the central zone and end zone as shown in the diagram.

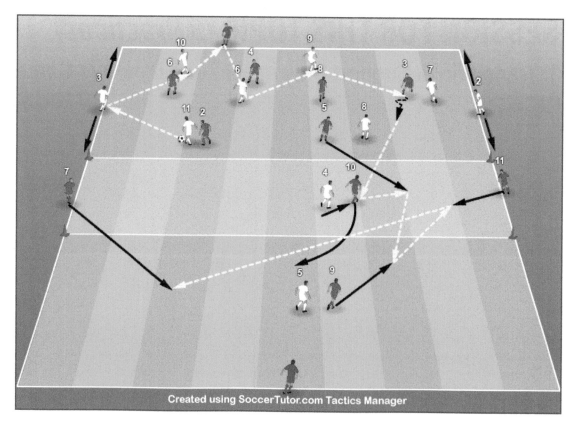

Created using SoccerTutor.com Tactics Manager

Once the ball reaches the end zone, the roles of the 2 teams changes. Now we have the situation as shown in the following diagram. The practice keeps going and now the whites aim to keep possession and get 1 point when they complete 6-8 passes. The aim for the red team is to steal the ball and pass quickly into the central zone to their Player 10 etc.

Rule:

The team that goes from defending to attacking have 1-2 touches in the first 2 zones and have unlimited touches in the final zone (except the 2 side players and neutral players who play with a maximum of 1 or 2 touches).

Coaching Points

1. The defending team use ball oriented defence to apply as much pressure as possible to win the ball back.

2. Defensive cover is needed to prevent possible passes and quick changes of defensive positions (transpose).

3. There should be the correct distances between the defenders when applying pressure.

4. In the transition from defence to attack, there needs to be good awareness, quick support and movement, quick decision making, a high tempo (1 touch football) and good communication.

PROGRESSION

2. Transition & Support Play with Side Players

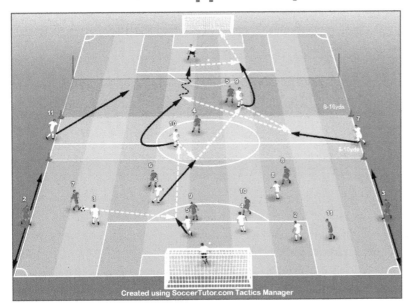

Description

Now we are using a full pitch. The team who are in transition from defence to attack now have a maximum of 8-10 seconds to finish their attack.

PROGRESSION

3. 11v11 Transition & Support Play in a 4 Zone Game

Description

Now the wide forwards (11 and 7) from the white team and the full backs (2 and 3) from the red team are playing inside the pitch from the beginning.

GOAL ANALYSIS
Exploiting the Weak Side of the Opposition (1)

10-Sep-11

Real Madrid 4-2 Getafe (3rd Goal): Benzema - Assist: Ronaldo

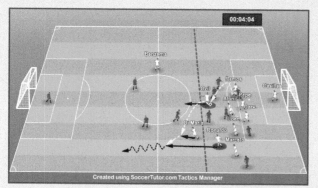

Ramos wins the ball from the opponent and passes to Ozil. With one touch, Ozil sees Di Maria and passes to him on the left. While the ball is travelling, Ronaldo sprints forward to support him. Di Maria passes to Ronaldo who dribbles forward with the ball at speed.

Now we have a 4v2 situation (+1 player tracking Ronaldo from behind) and Ronaldo sees Benzema's run on the weak side of the opponent and passes the ball in behind the last 2 defenders for Benzema to run onto

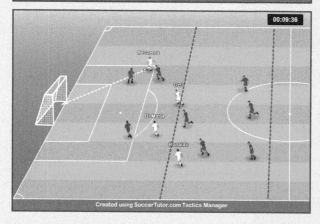

This example shows extremely good decision making and synchronisation (timing), both with Ronaldo's pass and Benzema's run. Benzema is quicker to the ball than the goalkeeper and with 1 touch scores the goal. The counter attack was completed in 9.36 seconds.

GOAL ANALYSIS
Exploiting the Weak Side of the Opposition (2)

02-May-12
Atletic Bilbao 0-3 Real Madrid (2nd Goal): Ozil - Assist: Ronaldo

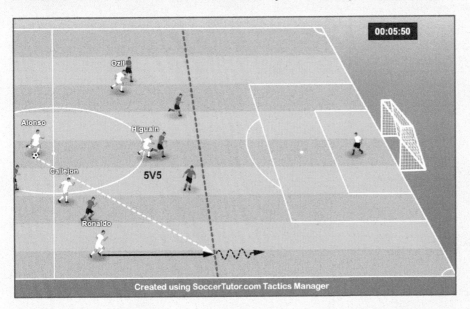

Real are again in a transition from defence to attack with a 5v5 situation. Alonso sees the free space on the right flank and hits a hard pass to Ronaldo, who dribbles the ball along the weak side of the opposition.

Ronaldo plays a cross/pass to the back post for Ozil in space and he is quickest to the ball before and scores with 1 touch. The attack was completed in 7.92 seconds.

SESSION FOR THIS TOPIC *(5 Practices)*
1. 3 Team Counter Attacking Small Sided Game

Created using SoccerTutor.com Tactics Manager

Objective

To develop transitions from defence to attack in the low zone and exploiting the weak side of the opponent.

Description

In an area 50 yards x 50 yards we divide into 2 equal grids. We have 2 teams of 7 and 6 extra neutral players in one of the halves. The red team, with the help of the neutrals try to score in the goal. The white team have a 4-2 formation using a ball oriented defence.

When the white team wins the ball they make a quick transition from defence to attack (with help from the neutral players who now play with them, but are not allowed to score). The neutral players at the side are not allowed to come inside.

The reds must make a quick transition from attack to defence. Once there is a goal scored, or the ball goes out, the drill starts from the other half and the 2 teams change roles. Also change roles for which team are the neutral players. From the time of winning the ball, the attack must be completed in 8 seconds. Limited touches for inside players and 1 or 2 touches for neutral players.

VARIATION

2. Dynamic 3 Team Counter Attacking Small Sided Game

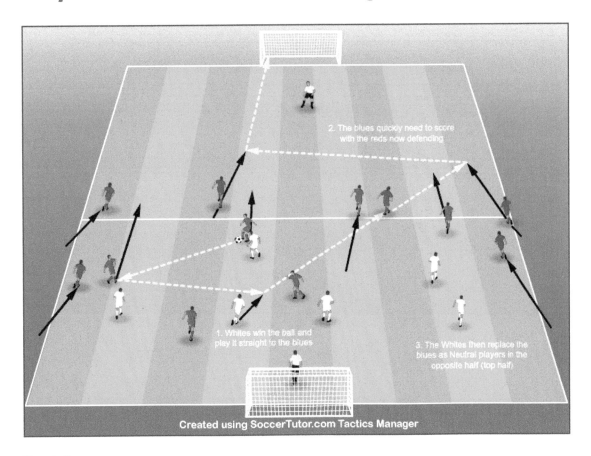

2. The blues quickly need to score with the reds now defending

1. Whites win the ball and play it straight to the blues

3. The Whites then replace the blues as Neutral players in the opposite half (top half)

Created using SoccerTutor.com Tactics Manager

Description

Here we have a variation. First, the red attack the whites. If the whites win the ball, they pass to the blues immediately and now the blues attack the reds at the other end (the whites become neutral).

If the ball goes out in this attack, the blues will then attack red in the top half with the whites as neutral. If the reds win the ball, they pass to the white team who attack the blues with support of the red team. The red team will then replace the whites as neutrals in the opposite half (bottom half).

Coaching Points

1. The defending team use ball oriented defence to apply as much pressure as possible to win the ball back.

2. In the transition from defence to attack, there needs to be an urgency to move the ball forward as quickly as possible while the other team have not had time to react.

3. There needs to be a number of forward runs into the attacking half to achieve a fast break attack.

4. During the transition to attack, they need to exploit the weak side of the opponent by using the full width.

PROGRESSION

3. Playing Wide and Switching Play in a Transition Game

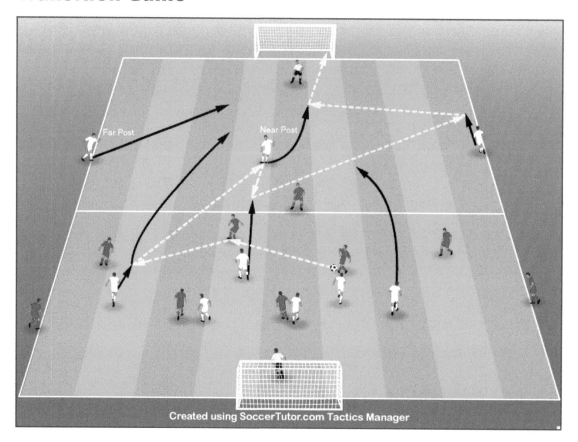

Created using SoccerTutor.com Tactics Manager

Objective

To develop transitions from defence to attack from the low zone with quick counter attacking combinations.

Description 10 v 10

In an area 50 yards x 50 yards, we divide into 2 halves again. In the first half we have 6 white defending players and a goalkeeper playing against 9 red players. The reds have 6 players inside the half and 3 extra players outside (2 on the sides and 1 on the middle line).

The red team aim is to score using their numerical advantage. If the white team win the ball, they quickly make a transition from defence to attack. They must get the ball to the white player in the middle of the attacking half as quickly as possible and he plays it back for a supporting runner. The ball should then be played wide to one of the white players near the sideline and the other 2 attacking players make near or far post runs respectively to finish on goal. The white players in the defending half must try to get forwards quickly to provide support.

The red players can only enter the other half once the ball is played in there. From the time of winning the ball, the attack must be completed in 8 seconds. If the ball goes out, the drill starts in the other half and they change roles.

PROGRESSION

4. Exploiting the Weak Side of the Opponent in a 3 Zone Transition Game

Created using SoccerTutor.com Tactics Manager

Objective

To develop transitions from defence to attack in the low zone and exploiting the weak side of the opponent.

Description 10 v 10

In an area 60 yards x 40 yards, we divide the pitch into 3 zones (20 yards x 40 yards each).

In the low zone, the white team are in a 4-2 formation defending against 7 attackers of the red team. If the white team wins the ball, they must pass quickly into the middle zone where they have a 4v3 numerical advantage. From the time the white team wins the ball, they have 10 seconds to finish their attack.

You can allow one defender to track back from the low zone, so we have a 4v3+1 situation in the transition (as shown in Real's 3rd goal against Getafe when Benzema scored).

PROGRESSION

5. Exploiting the Weak Side of the Opponent in a 3 Zone Transition Game using a Full Pitch

Created using SoccerTutor.com Tactics Manager

Objective

To develop transitions from defence to attack in the low zone and exploiting the weak side of the opponent.

Description

Using a full pitch now, we have 3 grids again. In the low zone there is a goalkeeper + 8 defenders vs 7 red attackers. In the middle zone we have a numerical disadvantage of 2v3 for the whites. When the whites win the ball and are in transition from defence to attack, a minimum 3 players from the low zone must move up to support the attack into the middle/high zones.

You can allow one more defender like the previous example so we have a 5v3+1 situation in the transition.

Alternatively, you can allow all players to take a full part in the transition phase (attackers and defenders can go into all zones once the ball is passed into the middle zone).

GOAL ANALYSIS

Long Pass to Switch Play to the Weak Side on the Break

29-Apr-12

Real Madrid 3-0 Sevilla (3rd Goal): Benzema - Assist: Ramos

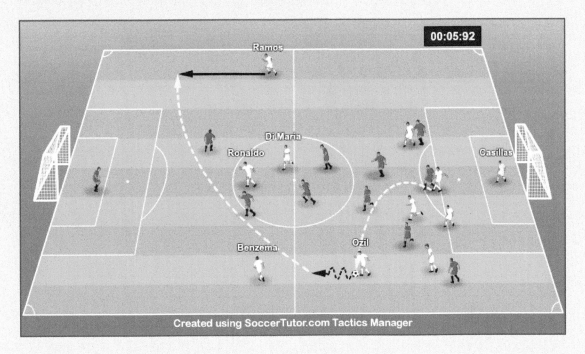

Ozil wins/receives the second ball and Real are in a positive transition with a numerical advantage to launch an attack.

Ozil has many options and chooses to exploit the weak side of the opposition with a long pass to change the direction of play.

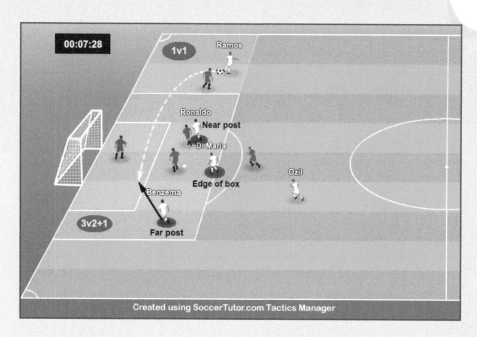

Ramos controls the pass on the right flank and crosses to the far post where Benzama has timed his run from the opposite flank. There were other options too as Ronaldo ran to the near post and Di Maria was coming in behind them.

Benzema shows good heading ability, scoring in the opposite corner. This counter attack took 9.04 seconds.

SESSION FOR THIS TOPIC *(2 Practices)*
1. Fast Break and Switch of Play in a 5 Zone Game (1)

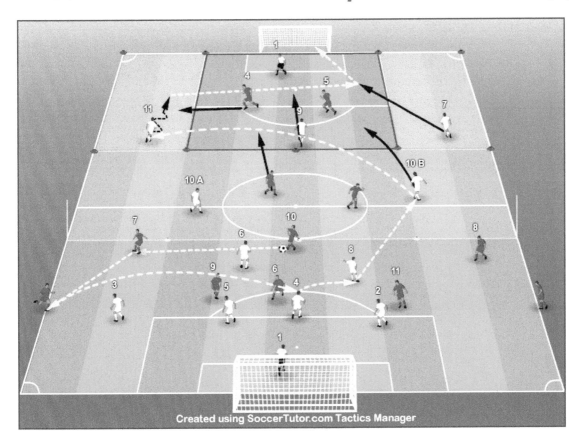

Created using SoccerTutor.com Tactics Manager

Objective

To develop transitions from defence to attack in the low zone and exploiting the weak side of the opponent.

Description

In this practice we use a full size pitch with 4 zones as shown in the diagram.

In the low zone we have a goalkeeper +6 white defenders against 6 red attackers +2 red outside players. The 6 whites are in a 4-2 formation and the reds have 4 midfielders and 2 attackers inside and 2 extra players at the sides.

The objective for the white team is to use good ball oriented defence and pass the ball quickly into the middle zone. In the middle zone there is a 2v2 situation. Middle players must receive the ball and pass very quickly to the wide forward on the opposite flank to them in the high zone.

Within the high zone, we have 2 side zones and 1 central zone (the box). When a side forward receives the ball they dribble the ball forwards until a central defender gets close to them and we have a 4v2+1 situation to finish the attack. From the time the white team wins the ball, they have 10 seconds to finish their attack.

VARIATION

2. Fast Break and Switch of Play in a 5 Zone Game (2)

Created using SoccerTutor.com Tactics Manager

Description

Here we have the same practice, but without the 2 outside players for the red team in the low zone.

GOAL ANALYSIS
Creating and Exploiting Space on the Flanks (1)

24-Sep-11
Real Madrid 6-2 Rayo Vallecano (1st Goal): Ronaldo - Assist: Ozil

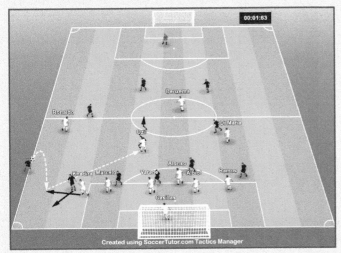

Khedira wins the ball from the opponent off a throw in (1v1 situation) and makes a quick pass to Ozil in the centre. Madrid are now in a positive transition and attack with a 4v4 situation. Ozil dribbles the ball forward.

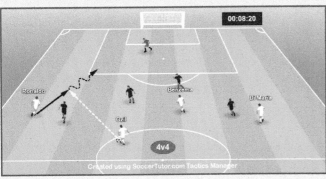

Ronaldo sprints up the left flank and wants the ball in the space. Ozil passes to him and Ronaldo demonstrates great speed and dribbling quality entering the penalty area.

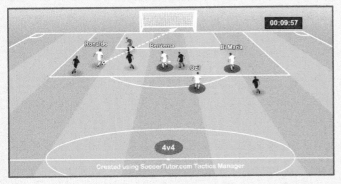

Ronaldo is too quick for the defenders and with the inside of his foot scores the goal. From the time that Khedira won the ball deep in his own half to Ronaldo scoring it only took 9.57 seconds.

GOAL ANALYSIS
Creating and Exploiting Space on the Flanks (2)

26-Oct-11

Real Madrid 3-0 Villareal (3ʳᵈ Goal): Di Maria - Assist: Benzema

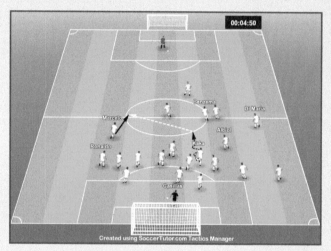

Here again we have a transition from defence to attack with Kaka taking the second ball and driving forward. He passes left to Marcelo.

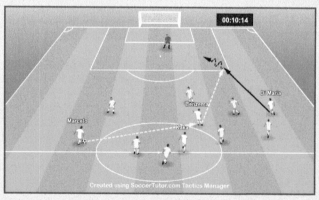

Marcelo passes back inside to Benzema and before the opposition defenders can get back into position, Benzema passes in behind them into the space on the right where Di Maria has made a forward run. He takes control of the ball and drives into the box.

Di Maria shapes the ball onto his left foot (his stronger foot) and with the inside of the foot, finishes into the opposite corner of the net. The attack took 11.70 seconds.

SESSION FOR THIS TOPIC *(5 Practices)*
GROUP 1

1. Defensive Organisation to Win Possession with Quick Break from the Low Zone

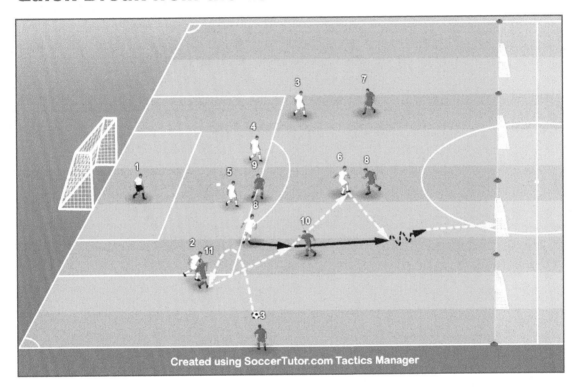

Created using SoccerTutor.com Tactics Manager

Objective
To develop defensive organisation in the low zone.

Description
In half a pitch we put 4 mini goals near the halfway line as shown in the diagram. One team (white) have a goalkeeper and 6 outfield players in a 4-2 formation. The attacking team (red) have 6 players. The practice starts from a throw in and the defenders immediately press the ball. If they win the ball, they must score in one of the mini goals within 6 seconds (quick transition from defence to attack).

Coaching Point
1. The defending team use ball oriented defence to apply as much pressure as possible to win the ball back.
2. Defensive cover is needed to prevent possible passes as well as quick changes of defensive positioning.
3. There should be the correct distances between the defenders when applying pressure.
4. In the transition from defence to attack, there needs to be good awareness, quick support and movement, quick decision making, a high tempo (1 touch football) and good communication.

GROUP 2

2. Fast Combinations, Support and Finishing Practice

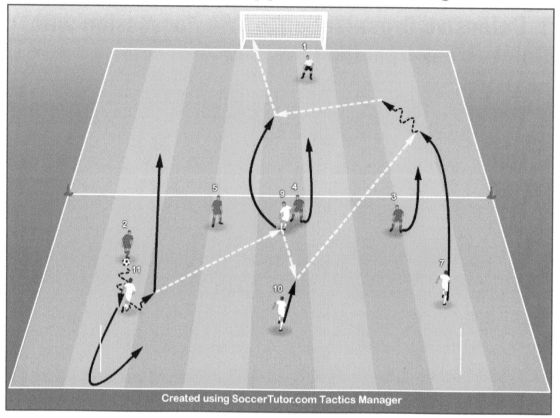

Created using SoccerTutor.com Tactics Manager

Objective

To develop quick transitions from defence to attack.

Description

In an area 30 yards x 25 yards, we divide the pitch into 2 grids. We have 4 defenders and 4 attackers (2 wide forwards, 1 attacking midfielder and 1 striker from the 4-2-3-1). The ball starts with the red right back who dribbles the ball up to the white No.11 and leaves the ball at his feet, sprints to the pole and around it to then defend the transition.

White 11 has taken the ball and dribbled forwards as the white team makes a quick transition to attack in a 4v3+1 situation (the +1 is the player who tracks after running round the pole). The attacking team must find the right solutions and combinations to score as the defending team try to stop them. The defenders are not allowed in the attacking half until the ball is played in there. Run the drill from both sides.

Coaching Point

1. A quick transition from defence to attack is needed.

2. Players should show good decision making and creativity at a high tempo (different passing combinations).

3. Runs in behind need to be correctly timed and coordinated to the direction and weight of pass.

GROUP 2 VARIATION

3. Fast Combinations, Support and Finishing Transition Game

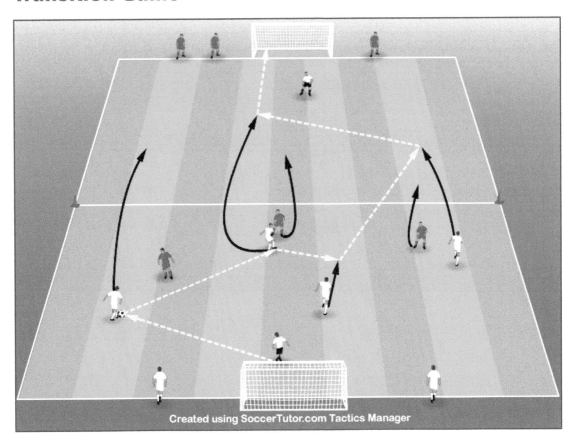

Created using SoccerTutor.com Tactics Manager

Description

In this variation the practice starts with the goalkeeper who passes to the side and the 4 white players launch a quick attack against the 3 red defenders. The defenders are not allowed in the other half before the ball is played in there.

When the attack is finished, 3 of the 4 white players switch places with the the 3 red players at the end. The 1 remaining white player is joined by the 2 white players from the other end and these 3 become the defenders.

The 3 red players who join the pitch are joined by 1 of the other 3 red players. The goalkeeper starts with the ball and the practice starts the same way but at the other end with the roles reversed.

PROGRESSION

4. Counter Attacking with a 4v3 Situation in a 3 Zone Game

Description

Using a full pitch we now combine the 2 groups into 1 drill and 1 group. The practice starts from a throw in the low zone where we have 6 outfield players (red) against 6 defenders + GK (white). The white team use a 1-4-2 formation and if they win the ball, they must quickly pass into the middle zone (maximum 4 seconds). In this zone there is a 4v3 situation. The aim is to launch a fast attack which should take a maximum of 10-12 seconds.

VARIATION

5. Counter Attacking with a 4v4 Situation in a 3 Zone Game

Description

We have the same drill here, but in the middle zone we have a 4v4 situation now.

GOAL ANALYSIS

Breaking from the Low Zone: Causing Imbalance in a Defensive Line with a Delayed Pass

28-Aug-11

Zaragoza 0-6 Real Madrid (4ᵗʰ Goal): Ronaldo - Assist: Di Maria

Marcelo steals the ball, passes to Ronaldo and then moves to support him with an overlapping run creating a 2v1 situation.

Ronaldo drives inside which causes the defence to become unbalanced as they move backwards.

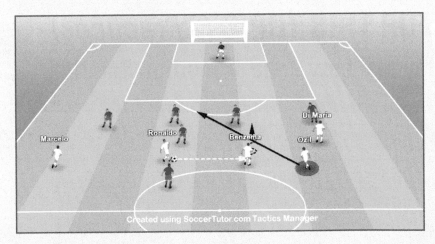

Ronaldo passes inside to Benzema. Benzema dribbles forward, carrying the ball up to the defensive line (making the centre back close him down). At the same time, Ozil makes an opposite diagonal cutting run at the back of the defensive line. This gives the opposition a problem and creates imbalance in their defence.

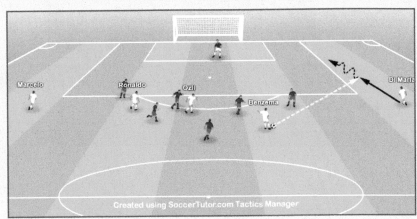

Benzema uses the space created by his and Ozil's movement and passes to Di Maria who has lots of space on the right flank. Di Maria dribbles forward and crosses low across the box (between the last defenders and the goalkeeper).

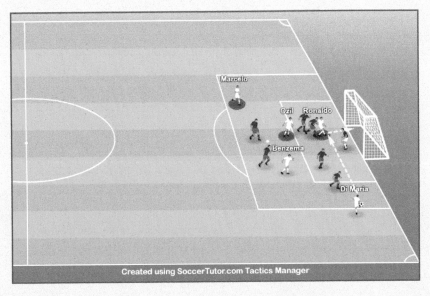

Ronaldo is quickest to the ball and with good timing receives the pass and scores the goal.

SESSION FOR THIS TOPIC *(2 Practices)*

1. Support Play in a Low Zone Transition Small Sided Game

Created using SoccerTutor.com Tactics Manager

Objective

To develop the transition play from defence to attack from the low zone - drawing players out of position to create imbalance in the opposition defence (and playing a delayed final ball to exploit space created).

Description

We divide a full pitch into 3 zones as shown in the diagram. The drill starts in the low zone where we have a goalkeeper +5 white defenders against 5 blue attackers. The white team use a 4-1 formation and the blues use a 4-1 or 3-2 formation.

The blues try to score and if 1 of the white players wins the ball, their objective is to pass into the middle zone to a teammate coming down from the high zone (unmarked) and then provide quick support using a 1-2 combination as displayed (1 blue player follows). We now have a 5v5 situation in the opposite zone and the blue team are in the defensive phase and the drill continues. Players are not marked in the middle zone.

Coaching Points

1. The use of 1-2 combinations are key as a way of practicing moving up the pitch on the break from the low zone.
2. Encourage players to dribble forwards with the ball close to their feet up to the defensive line and then play a delayed pass (draws defenders out of position and creates space behind to exploit).
3. There needs to be good coordination of the final ball and the timing of the run in behind.

PROGRESSION

2. Fast Break Attacks in Behind the Defensive Line in a Low Zone Transition Game

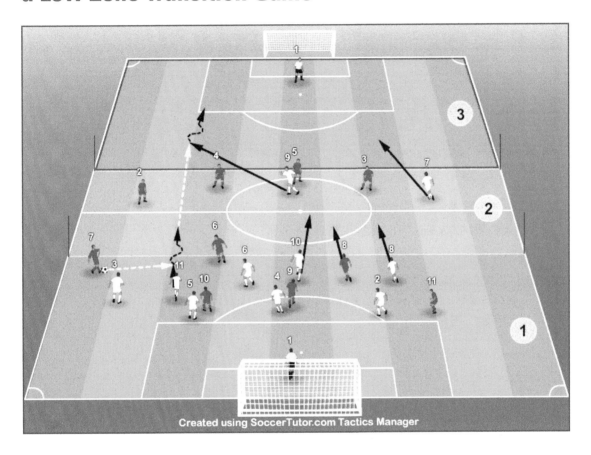

Created using SoccerTutor.com Tactics Manager

Description

Now in the low zone we have 8 whites and 6 blue. In the middle zone we have a 2v4 situation.

When the whites win the ball, 3 players can move up from the low zone (+1 blue player can move out to track) creating a 5v4+1 situation. When the attack is finished, the drill starts again from the opposite side and the teams change roles.

CHAPTER 5

THE TRANSITION FROM DEFENCE TO ATTACK IN THE MIDDLE ZONE

Goal Analysis: Breaking from the Middle Zone:
Causing Imbalance in a Defensive Line with a Delayed Pass 162
SESSION FOR THIS TOPIC *(3 Practices)*
1. Win the Ball, Dribble, Delayed Final Ball and Finish...164
2. Win the Ball, Dribble and Delayed Pass in an Opposed Practice 165
3. Win the Ball, Dribble and Delayed Pass against a High Line 166

Goal Analysis: Winning Possession in the Centre: Breaking vs a High Line 167
SESSION FOR THIS TOPIC *(3 Practices)*
1. Interceptions and Fast Counter Attacking in a 3 Zone Game...171
2. Fast Counter Attacking from the Middle Zone (1) 172
3. Fast Counter Attacking from the Middle Zone (2) 173

Goal Analysis: Overload Fast Break Attack...174
SESSION FOR THIS TOPIC *(3 Practices)*
1. 2v2 / 3v2 Defence to Attack Transition Duel Game...175
2. Fast Break Attacks in a 2 Zone Support Play Game 177
3. 3v2 Support Play in an Attacking / Defending Duel Game 178

THE TRANSITION FROM DEFENCE TO ATTACK IN THE MIDDLE ZONE

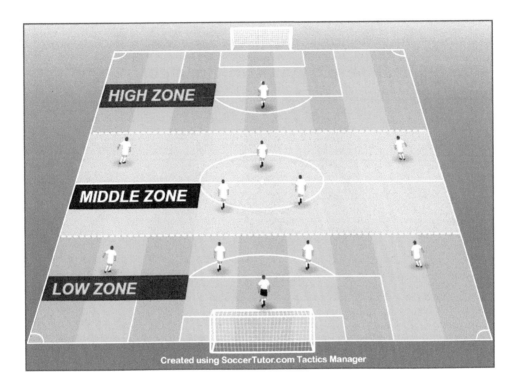

1. In the first case we have the opponent losing possession in the centre and then a Real player dribbling the ball up the pitch on the break. Usually in these cases, the opponent had 4 players behind the ball and their defence would be a large distance away from the other players. Real would enter into a transition to attack in a 4v4 situation and the objective is for the player with the ball was to dribble up to the defensive line and for the other players to make diagonal runs in behind the defensive line to receive the ball and score.

2. Many teams who lost possession in the middle zone kept a high defensive line, but Real Madrid were extremely strong in this situation and could recognise the situation immediately knowing exactly how to exploit it. The objective was to exploit the players' speed and attack the space in behind the defensive line. The player who won the ball would make a quick pass making sure to retain possession and the second player would like to make the final pass into space for an oncoming runner.

3. We also had situations where the opposition were imbalanced when they lost possession and had many players in front of the ball, with only 2 or 3 players behind the ball. In this case Real would make a fast break attack with an overload to create situations like 2+1v2 or 3+1v3. This was an easy situation for a team of Real's calibre to exploit in the transition from defence to attack. The timing of the upcoming runner from deep (+1) and the timing of the pass into space for this spare man was key to Real's success in these situations (creating a numerical advantage in the high zone).

GOAL ANALYSIS

Breaking from the Middle Zone: Causing Imbalance in a Defensive Line with a Delayed Pass

28-Aug-11

Zaragoza 0-6 Real Madrid (1st Goal): Ronaldo - Assist: Ozil

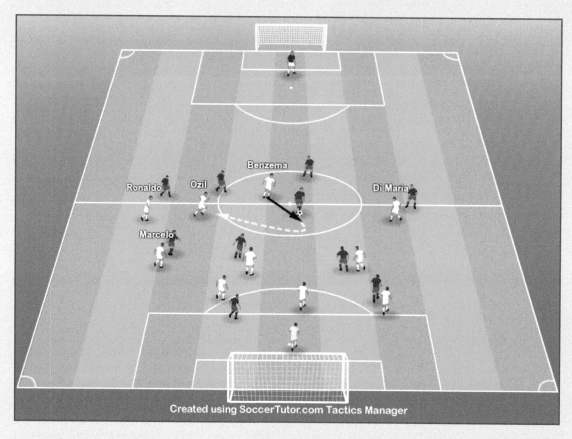

Benzema presses the opponent from behind and steals the ball in the centre. Real enter the transition phase with a 4v4 situation.

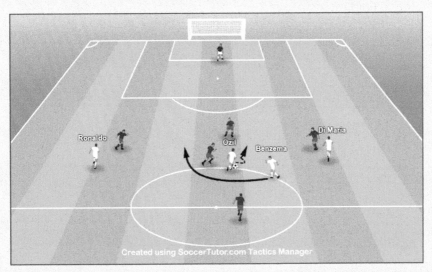

Benzema makes an inside left overlap and Ozil dribbles to the right.

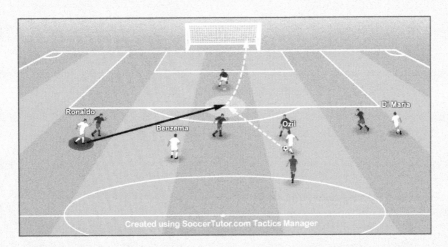

Ozil dribbles the ball up to his opponent drawing him in. Ronaldo recognises this situation and makes a run in behind the defensive line (between the right back and the centre back).

Ozil plays a good pass into the space for Ronaldo to score past the goalkeeper.

SESSION FOR THIS TOPIC *(3 Practices)*
1. Win the Ball, Dribble, Delayed Final Ball and Finish

Created using SoccerTutor.com Tactics Manager

Objective

To develop the transition play from defence to attack from the middle zone - drawing players out of position to create imbalance in the opposition defence (and playing a delayed final ball to exploit space created).

Description

On 3 quarters of a pitch, we create a grid with 3 mini goals at one end as shown (44 x 34 yards). There is a 4v4 situation, the white team has 4 attacking players from the 4-2-3-1 and the blue team have 4 defenders. The coach plays a long pass to the blue defenders and the white team immediately press to their opponents who are trying to score in the 3 mini goals.

If the white team win the ball they start a transition from defence to attack and must get out of the grid (the blues must stay in the grid). In the final zone, we have 4 mannequins and 1 of the white attackers dribbles the ball up to them and his teammates look to move into the space behind the back 4 (mannequins), to receive the pass and finish.

Coaching Points

1. The white players need to press as a unit to limit space and time and win the ball quickly.
2. In the transition to attack the passes and dribbling should be at a high tempo with 1 touch combinations and finishing.
3. The rhythm and timing of the movement and passing needs to be coordinated to break effectively.

PROGRESSION

2. Win the Ball, Dribble and Delayed Pass in an Opposed Practice

Description

The same as the previous, but we now have 4 real defenders in the final zone

Different rules:

1. The 4 defenders are only passive.

2. The 4 defenders are active, but cannot intercept the ball while it is travelling.

3. The 4 defenders are fully active.

PROGRESSION

3. Win the Ball, Dribble and Delayed Pass against a High Line

Created using SoccerTutor.com Tactics Manager

Description

The area is now 40 yards x 40 yards and we have a 6v6. Both teams now have 2 central midfielders (6 & 8).

If the white team wins the ball, they attack and play a pass in behind the defensive line and try to score in the final zone.

The blue defenders are not allowed in the final zone until the ball is played in there.

Progression

The blue defenders are allowed in the final zone before the ball is played in there.

GOAL ANALYSIS
Winning Possession in the Centre: Breaking vs a High Line (1)

10-Mar-12

Real Betis 2-3 Real Madrid (1st Goal): Higuain - Assist: Di Maria

Khedira wins the 1v1 with the opponent and passes to Di Maria. Real Madrid go into a transition from defence to attack. The opposition keep a high line and Di Maria gains some yards dribbling forward with the ball.

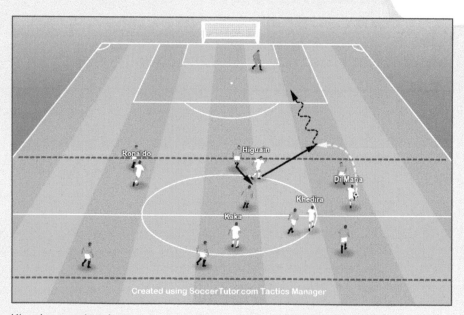

Higuain recognises the situation and makes a diagonal run round the back of the left back. Di Maria passes to him in the space and Higuain receives behind the defenders and takes advantage by driving towards the box.

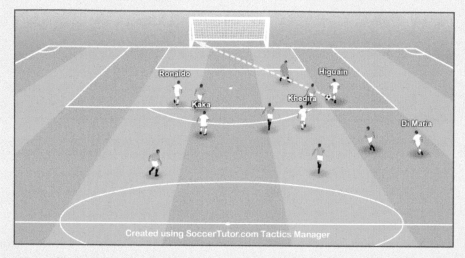

Higuain finishes in the far corner of the net.

GOAL ANALYSIS
Winning Possession in the Centre:
Breaking vs a High Line (2)

21-Apr-12
Barcelona 1-2 Real Madrid (2nd Goal): Ronaldo - Assist: Ozil

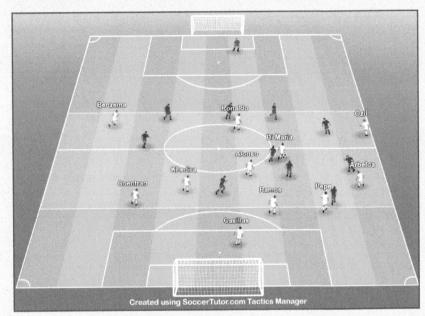

Real win the ball in the centre of the pitch and Di Maria dribbles the ball forward. He has 5 opponents behind him and 4 in front of him (+ 3 teammates).

The opposition left back makes a mistake by leaving his position to close down Di Maria. This leaves an easy pass to Ozil who is free on the right.

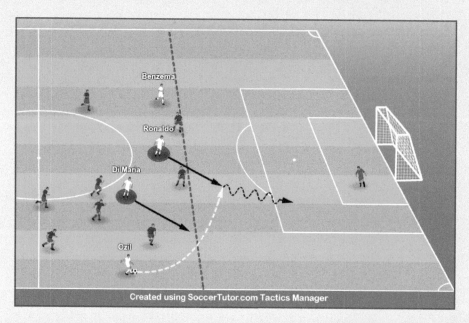

Created using SoccerTutor.com Tactics Manager

Ozil has a lot of free space to run into, but does not want to allow the pposition time to get back into position. He sees the diagonal runs of Di Maria and Ronaldo. He plays the pass to Ronaldo in behind the defensive line who has plenty of space to take advantage of

Created using SoccerTutor.com Tactics Manager

Ronaldo is quickest and receives the ball, dribbles round the goalkeeper and scores the goal.

SESSION FOR THIS TOPIC *(3 Practices)*

1. Interceptions and Fast Counter Attacking in a 3 Zone Game

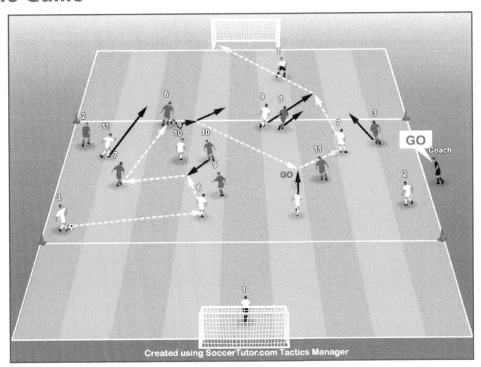

Created using SoccerTutor.com Tactics Manager

Objective

To practice winning the ball in the middle zone and launching very fast counter attacks.

Description 9 v 9

In an area 60 yards x 40 yards we divide the pitch into 3 grids. We have 1 central zone which is 30 yards x 40 yards and 2 final zones which are 15 yards x 40 yards. Both teams use a 2-2-3-1 formation.

The drill starts in the central zone where both teams have the objective to keep possession of the ball to get 1 point after completing 6-8 passes.

The coach waits for a point where a team has lost possession and shouts 'GO' - the team that has just won the ball then makes a quick transition to attack and must try to score in the opposition's goal (within 3-4 touches or 4-6 seconds). The other team must make a quick transition to defend.

Coaching Points

1. Both teams need to try and keep possession under pressure.

2. When one team wins the ball from the opponent and the coach shouts 'Go' the players need to react very quickly to the situation and demonstrate good decision making, movement and intelligent runs.

3. This practice should be done at a high tempo, with accurate passes, good communication and very quick finishing.

PROGRESSION

2. Fast Counter Attacking from the Middle Zone (1)

Safe zone for the blues in possession

Created using SoccerTutor.com Tactics Manager

Description 8 v 9

Using a full pitch, we create an area which is 40 yards x 65 yards and put 4 mini goals at one end. The white team are using a 2-2-3-1 formation and the blues are in a 4-4 formation.

The drill starts with the blue goalkeeper and the blue team then try to score in the 4 mini goals (1 point). The white players are not allowed in the high/safe zone when the opposition have the ball, so they must stay in the main area and then press when the ball is played in there.

The white team's objective is to win the ball and make a very quick transition from defence to attack (and get in behind the defensive line and score in the high zone).

Rules:

1. White players have limited touches and blue players have unlimited touches.

2. The white team has 4-5 sec or 3-4 touches to move the ball from the middle zone to the high zone.

PROGRESSION

3. Fast Counter Attacking from the Middle Zone (2)

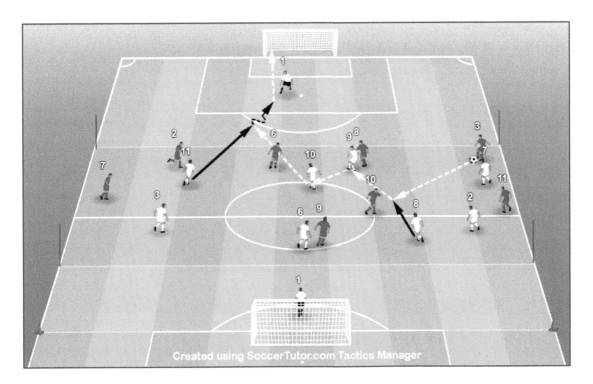

Created using SoccerTutor.com Tactics Manager

Description 9 v 9

In this progression we now play with 9v9 and we have a full size goal at both ends. The objectives are the same.

The drill always starts with the blue team. The white team start to press as soon as the ball enters the middle zone.

The 2 teams change roles after 10 minutes.

GOAL ANALYSIS
Overload Fast Break Attack

17-Dec-11

Sevilla 2-6 Real Madrid (6th Goal): Altintop - Assist: Alonso

Real are on a fast break attack with a 2v2 situation. Altintop dribbles the ball inside from the left.

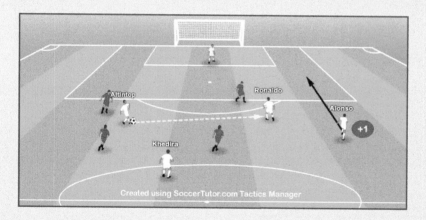

Altintop passes the ball inside to Ronaldo. Alonso has made a run up from the back and Real have a numerical advantage with a 3v2 situation. This provides Ronaldo with an extra option.

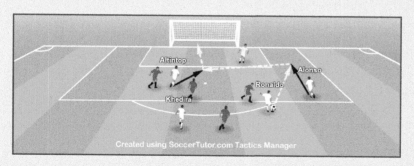

Ronaldo dribbles the ball up to the defender and at the correct time passes to Alonso in the space on the right. Alonso plays a first time cross to Altintop who has made a run into the box from the other side and scores with 1 touch.

SESSION FOR THIS TOPIC *(3 Practices)*

1. 2v2 / 3v2 Defence to Attack Transition Duel Game

Objective

To develop fast break attacks with an overload of runners (creating a numerical advantage).

Description

In an area 25 yards x 25 yards we use 2 full size goals. We have 2 teams with 6 players each. The drill starts with the goalkeeper of one team and there is a 2v2 situation outfield.

When the coach instructs, a 3rd player from the team in possession runs quickly to join and create a numerical advantage (3v2 situation). To progress the drill this can work without the coach's instruction being needed.

When the attack is finished the goalkeeper from the other team passes the ball out to his 2 players who then attack the other goal. At this time, a 3rd player from their team runs from the outside line to support them and create a 3v2 situation again.

Every time one of the attacks is finished, one of the 3 attacking players goes to the sideline and the other 2 stay on to defend.

Coaching Points

1. The players on the side need to be fully concentrated so they can offer quick support.

2. Encourage creativity for the different attacking combinations.

3. One player should always be able to run into space and receive as there is a 3v2 numerical advantage.

4. Focus on the accuracy and weight of pass - good final balls should be into space for the spare player to run onto and finish with 1 touch.

PROGRESSION

2. Fast Break Attacks in a 2 Zone Support Play Game

Created using SoccerTutor.com Tactics Manager

Description

In an area 30 yards x 30 yards, we divide the pitch into 2 halves with 2 full size goals.

We have 2 teams and the drill starts with the goalkeeper of one team who then passes to an outfield player and we have a 2v2 situation in each half.

The objective is to pass to their 2 teammates in the attacking half and quickly move up to support them and create a numerical advantage (3v2). If the attack is finished or the ball goes out, then immediately 1 player from the attacking half goes out and 1 player comes inside (as shown in diagram) and the drill continues as both teams changes roles.

Coaching Points

1. Players have to demonstrate close control and strength in the 1v1 or 2v2 situations.

2. Decision making is important - whether to hold the ball, beat the defender or pass to a teammate in space.

3. When a pass is made into the attacking half, that player needs to sprint forwards quickly to provide support and create a numerical advantage 3v2.

VARIATION

3. 3v2 Support Play in an Attacking / Defending Duel Game

Created using SoccerTutor.com Tactics Manager

Description

In an area 30 yards x 30 yards, we divide into 2 halves again with 2 full size goals. We have 4 defenders and 7-8 attackers.

The drill starts with the goalkeeper who passes to 1 of the 2 defenders who are against 1 attacker in this half. Their aim is to pass to an attacker in the other half. At this point, 1 more attacker enters from the side and makes a 3v2 situation (whichever side the ball is closest too is the side where the player comes from). The aim is to use the 3v2 advantage to combine and score very quickly.

When the attack is finished or the ball goes out, only 1 attacker stays in the top half and the drill continues with the goalkeeper and a 2v1 situation again. The other 2 attackers leave the pitch.

In the bottom half, 1 player joins from the side and there is a 2v2 situation again. The same sequence is repeated, but from the opposite side.

CHAPTER 6

THE TRANSITION FROM DEFENCE TO ATTACK IN THE HIGH ZONE

Goal Analysis: Transition from Attack to Defence & then Defence to Attack 181
SESSION FOR THIS TOPIC *(4 Practices)*
1. Passing, Pressing and Fast Break in an Unopposed Practice...184
2. Possession, Winning the Ball and Counter Attacking in a Dynamic Game (1)..186
3. Counter Attacking in a Dynamic Game (2)...188
4. Counter Attacking in a Dynamic Game (3)...188

THE TRANSITION FROM DEFENCE TO ATTACK IN THE HIGH ZONE

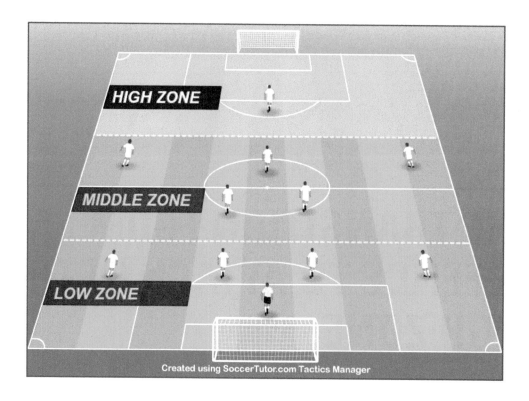

Created using SoccerTutor.com Tactics Manager

Here we analyse what happened when Real Madrid went into a transition from defence to attack in the high zone and very close to the opposition's penalty area.

This would normally occur when Real were attacking using safe possession and were trying to find attacking solutions against an opponent with an organised defence in the high zone and lost the ball.

They would immediately move to press the player in possession denying them time and space. This was done at a very high tempo to create a transition from defence to attack in the high zone.

The objective in this situation was to exploit the imbalance in the defensive line that has not had time to react.

The player who won the ball would look to immediately play a forward pass to a teammate in a better position close to the penalty area. The attack would normally be concluded in a maximum of 6 seconds.

GOAL ANALYSIS
Transition from Attack to Defence & then Defence to Attack (1)
06-Nov-11
Real Madrid 7-1 Osasuna (7th Goal): Benzema - Assist: Arbeloa

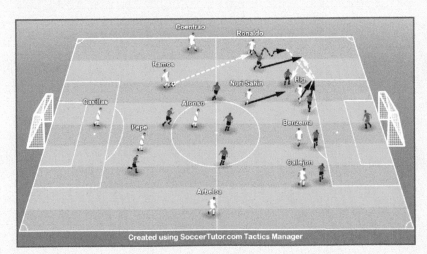

Real attack from the left and Ronaldo tries to combine with Higuain. The ball is won by the opponent and Real move very quickly to a transition from attack to defence.

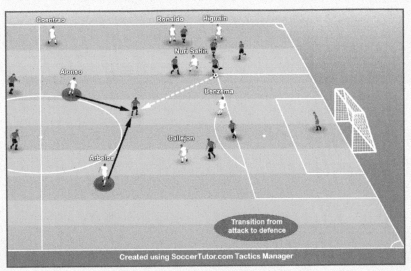

The opposition player is under pressure and has limited time and space and passes to the central midfielder in the centre. As the ball is travelling to him, Arbeloa and Alonso move up and close him down. They do not allow him to turn, preventing him from being able to dribble or pass.

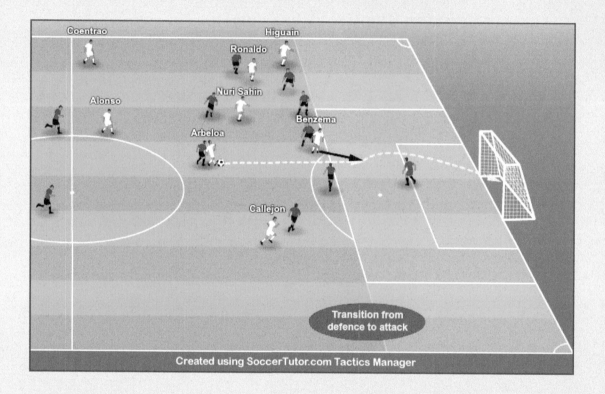

Arbeloa wins the ball and passes quickly to Benzema (quick transition from defence to attack). Benzema, as the defence have not had time to react and are imbalanced, receives the pass from Arbeloa and scores past the goalkeeper.

GOAL ANALYSIS

Transition from Attack to Defence & then Defence to Attack (2)

04-Mar-12

Real Madrid 5-0 Espanyol (1st Goal): Ronaldo - Assist: Higuain

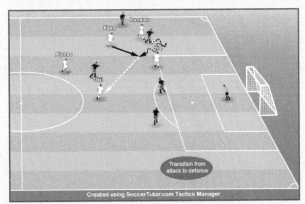

Real lose possession in the high zone and quickly move from attacking to defending with a high press of the opponent player in possession. He is under pressure with limited time and space. He makes a bad pass straight to Ozil and Real move from pressing/defending to attacking now.

We have the same situation as the previous one and Ozil passes quickly to Higuain who takes up a good position in an imbalanced defensive line and as he is closed down by the centre back, passes the ball to Ronaldo on the outside.

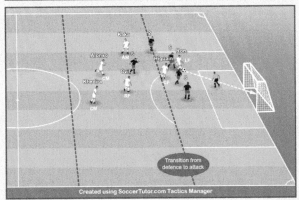

Ronaldo finishes well with his first touch.

SESSION FOR THIS TOPIC *(4 Practices)*

1. Passing, Pressing and Fast Break in an Unopposed Practice

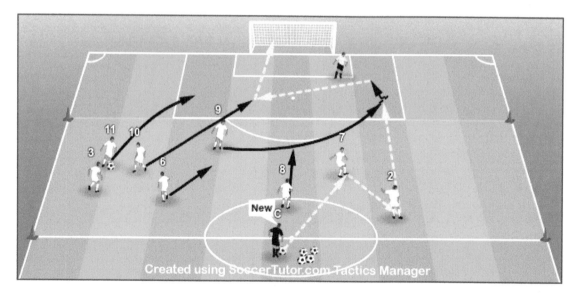

Objective

To develop the transition from attack to defence and then quickly from defence to attack.

Description

We create a zone from the edge of the penalty area to the halfway line. 8 players play with unopposed possession in formation (2-2-3-1).

They wait for the coach who orders the player who has possession of the ball to become the opponent and all the other players make a quick transition from attack to defence and immediately press him, but without taking the ball (only taking up the correct positions for the situation).

With the second order from the coach, he plays a new ball into a different player and now all the team make a quick transition from defence to attack. The attack must finish in 5-6 seconds.

Coaching Points

1. Players need to pass the ball around maintaining their respective positions in the formation and be prepared for the transition to defence (pressing the man in possession).

2. When the coach passes the second ball in all players need to make a quick transition to attack, making forward passes and well timed runs into the box.

PROGRESSION

2. Possession, Winning the Ball and Counter Attacking in a Dynamic Game (1)

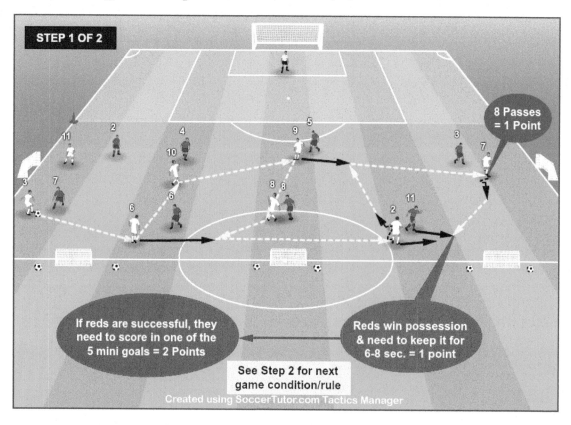

Description 8 v 8 (+GK)

In the same area, we put 3 mini goals on the halfway line and 2 mini goals on the sidelines as shown (these goals help develop the transition to defence as you have to close the player very quickly and prevent them using their stronger foot).

The white team is in a 2-2-3-1 formation and the red team are in a 4-4 formation.

The drill starts with the white team in possession and the first objective is to keep possession of the ball under the pressure from the opponent. If they complete 8 passes they get 1 point.

If the red team wins the ball, the second objective for the white team is to win it back within 6-8 seconds. If they are unable to do this, the red team wins 1 point and if the red team manages to score in one of the 5 mini goals they get 2 points.

The white team win possession & must finish on goal within 6-10 sec. = 2 points

When the white team win back possession, their third objective is to attack and score in the goal with the goalkeeper within 6-10 seconds (Step 2 of 2 Diagram). They get 2 points if they score.

The white team play with unlimited touches when in possession in the first objective. When they win the ball in the third objective they are limited to 1-2 touches.

Coaching Points

1. The practice should develop very quick transitions to press/defend when possession is lost. It should also develop very quick transitions to attack when possession is won back.

2. In the transition from defence to attack there needs to be good decision making under pressure of space and time.

3. This practice develops the team's ability to keep possession under pressure with limited time and space.

4. Correct body shape (open up and half turn) and positioning is important to view the options for where the next pass is going.

5. Checking away from the marker before moving to receive the ball is especially important to create space in tight areas.

6. Decision making is key - when to pass to feet, when to pass into space, the weight of pass and the timing and direction of runs in behind.

VARIATION
3. Counter Attacking in a Dynamic Game (2)

Description: The same us the previous one but we remove the 2 mini goals on the sideline.

PROGRESSION
4. Counter Attacking in a Dynamic Game (3)

Description: We remove the 3 mini goals and put a full size goal on the halfway line.

CHAPTER 7

BUILDING UP PLAY FROM THE LOW ZONE TO THE HIGH ZONE

Goal Analysis: Passing Through the Midfield Line from the Back 191
SESSION FOR THIS TOPIC (*5 Practices*)
1. Possession & Forward Passing in a 3 Zone Dynamic Game...193
2. 6v6 (+2) Possession & Forward Passing in a 3 Zone Dynamic Game 194
3. Passing Through the Midfield Line Transition Game 195
4. Passing Through the Midfield Line in a 3 Team Dynamic Transition Game 196
5. Passing Through Midfield Line & Finishing in a 5 Zone Game 197

Goal Analysis: Building Up Play from the Back Through the Centre 198
SESSION FOR THIS TOPIC (*2 Practices*)
1. 9v9 (+2) Position Specific 5 Zone Possession Game 201
2. Building Up Play from the Back in 1v1 / 2v2 / 3v3 Zones..203

Goal Analysis: Build Up Play with a 4v4 Situation on the Flank 204
PRACTICE FOR THIS TOPIC
1. Building Up Play From the Back with a 4v4 Central Zone...205

Goal Analysis: Creating 1v1 and 2v1 Situations Near the Penalty Area 206
SESSION FOR THIS TOPIC (*3 Practices*)
1. 'End to End' 3v3 (+3) Possession Game...207
2. 'End to End' 5v5 (+1) Possession Game...208
3. Build Up Through the Centre and Support Play in a 9 Zone Dynamic 10v10 Game.................209

BUILDING UP PLAY FROM THE LOW ZONE TO THE HIGH ZONE

In this situation we have Real Madrid building up their attack from the back and they must find solutions depending on:

a)   The formation of the opponent

b)   Where and how the opposition start to defend and press the ball

c)   What area the opposition is weak:

- As individuals

- As a group

- As a team

As we will see in this chapter, Real Madrid attack with the an emphasis on a relatively direct game with forward passing. They looked to work the ball very quickly forward to get in behind the defensive line of the opposition.

The objective in the first phase of attack was to bypass the attacking and midfield lines of the opposition using direct forward passes in behind them, thus eliminating numerous players from the game.

When this happened Real would have 4 or 5 players against the last defensive line of the opponent and then in the second and the third phase of the attack would use the combinations analysed in all our previous examples.

It is very clear that Real Madrid and Jose Mourinho work very hard on these phases on the training ground. They are extremely quick to recognise specific situations during a match. They display very good decision making and their success usually depended on the energy and speed of the opposition they were up against.

GOAL ANALYSIS
Passing Through the Midfield Line from the Back (1)
17-Dec-11
Sevilla 2-6 Real Madrid (1ˢᵗ Goal): Ronaldo - Assist: Di Maria

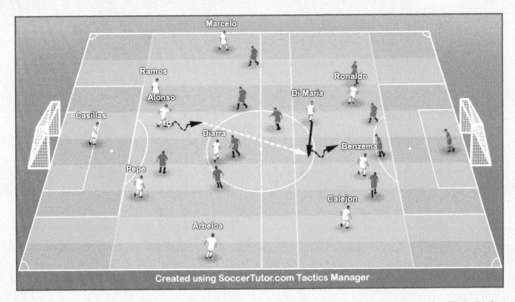

Created using SoccerTutor.com Tactics Manager

Real Madrid start their attack from the back against an opponent using a 4-1-4-1 formation. Sevilla hold their lines to defend and don't press the player with the ball. The distances between the lines is big and Real looked to exploit this. Ramos and Pepe open up at the edge of the box, and the full backs provide width as Alonso dribbles the ball forwards and passes to Di Maria who shows excellent movement to receive behind the midfield line. Alonso, with 1 pass from the back takes 6 players out of the game. Di Maria has a quality directional first touch, turns and dribbles the ball at the back 4 who are very deep.

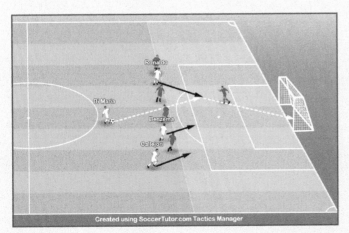

Created using SoccerTutor.com Tactics Manager

Sevilla's back 4 plays in a straight line and Ronaldo and Benzema make runs in between the full backs and centre backs.

Di Maria plays a great pass to Ronaldo in behind the back 4 and into space in the penalty area and he finishes into the far post.

GOAL ANALYSIS
Passing Through the Midfield Line from the Back (2)

10-Mar-12

Real Betis 2-3 Real Madrid (2nd Goal): Ronaldo - Assist: Marcelo

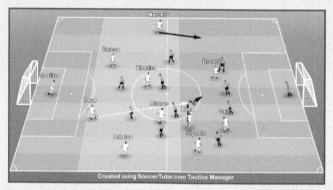

We have the same situation again here. Real Betis were using the 4-4-2 formation but again there is a distance between the lines to exploit and they do not pressure the player with the ball. Pepe passes to Kaka who makes a very clever run in behind the midfield line and takes 6 players out of the game. Kaka takes the ball forward and we have a 4v4 situation.

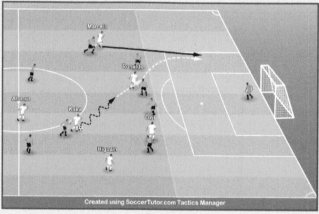

Kaka dribbles the ball inside and tries to play Ronaldo through with a chip pass.

The defender blocks the pass with his head and sends the ball to the left where Marcelo is able to get to the ball first.

Marcelo plays the ball across from the left and Ronaldo makes a movement to the near post and scores. 3 other Real players were also running into the box in the correct space and at the right time.

SESSION FOR THIS TOPIC *(5 Practices)*

1. Possession & Forward Passing in a 3 Zone Dynamic Game

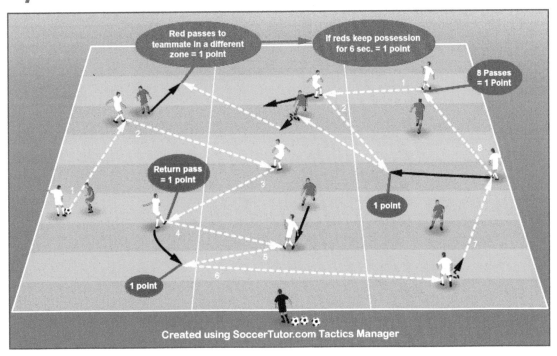

Created using SoccerTutor.com Tactics Manager

Objective

To develop possession in zones and playing forward passes through defensive lines (creating a numerical advantage in the final third).

Description

In an area 30 yards x 15 yards, divide the pitch into 3 equal zones. In each zone we have a 3v2 situation for the white team. The objective is to keep possession of the ball and play passes from one outside zone to the other outside zone. All players (from both teams) must stay in their zones. The white team can win 1 point when they complete 8 passes and 2 points if the ball goes from one outside zone to the other and back again.

If the red team win the ball, the whites must make a quick transition to defence and the 3 white players in that zone must try to win the ball back immediately. If the red team manage to pass to a teammate in another zone they get 1 point. Also, if the white team does not manage to win the ball back within 6 seconds the red team get 1 point. Limit the white players to either 1 touch or 2 touches.

Coaching Points

1. This practice develops the team's ability to keep possession under pressure with limited time and space.

2. Correct body shape (open up and half turn) and positioning is important to view the options for where the next pass is going.

VARIATION

2. 6v6 (+2) Possession & Forward Passing in a 3 Zone Dynamic Game

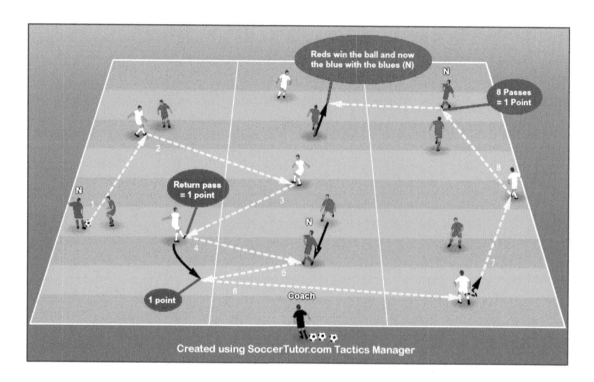

Description

The same as the previous drill, but now we have an extra neutral player (blue) in each grid. The neutral players play with whichever team has possession.

If the red team wins the ball, the reds and whites change roles. The red team go into a transition from defence to attack and the whites from attack to defence.

PROGRESSION

3. Passing Through the Midfield Line Transition Game

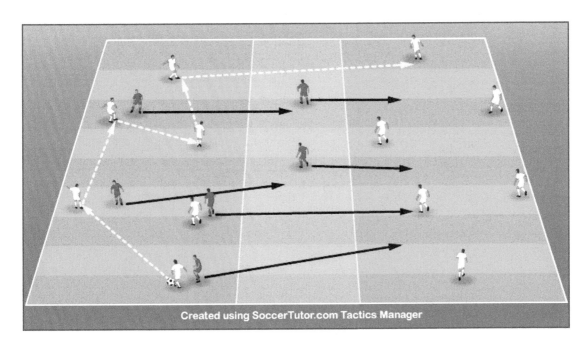

Created using SoccerTutor.com Tactics Manager

Objective

To develop possession in zones and playing forward passes through defensive lines (creating a numerical advantage in the attacking half).

Description

In an area 60 yards x 30 yards we have 3 zones. The central zone is 10 yards x 30 yards and the 2 outside zones are 25 yards x 30 yards. In the left outside zone we have a 6v4 situation for the white team. There are also 2 red players in the middle zone and 6 other whites in the other outside zone.

The whites keep possession and must first aim to complete 5 passes and then try to pass the ball to the opposite zone to get 1 point. You can progress the drill by removing the need to complete the 5 passes, encouraging direct early passes. The 2 red players in the middle try to intercept the passes. If the pass is successful, the 2 red players from the middle zone and 2 red players from the other zone run quickly across to apply pressure on the ball making it 4 red players again vs the 6 white players who have possession on the other side.

If the white team lose possession in the outside zone, they make a quick transition from attack to defence with a 6v4 advantage.

If one of the 2 red players in the middle zone intercept the ball, the 6 white players play against all 6 red players in a bigger area which now includes the middle zone. The 2 red middle players must still stay in their zone, but all the other players are able to move freely in both zones. The aim for the whites is to win the ball back very quickly. Limit the white players to either 1 or 2 touches.

VARIATION

4. Passing Through the Midfield Line in a 3 Team Dynamic Transition Game

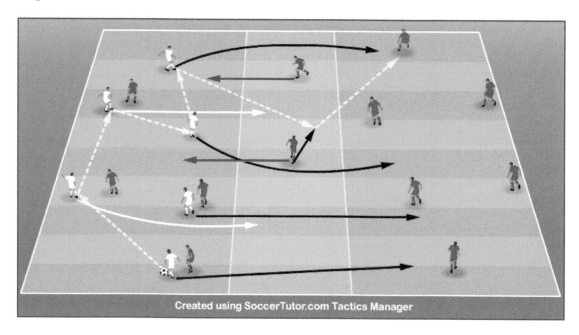

Created using SoccerTutor.com Tactics Manager

Description

In this progression, we now we have 3 teams of 6. 2 teams are trying to keep possession and the other team is in the defensive phase.

If the defending team wins the ball, they pass to the team in the opposite outside zone. Then all 6 players on the team move to the vacant outside zone.

The team that lost possession make a quick transition from attack to defence. 4 players move to the opposite outside zone to press the ball and the other 2 move into the middle zone to try and intercept any passes to the other outside zone.

PROGRESSION

5. Passing Through the Midfield Line & Finishing in a 5 Zone Game

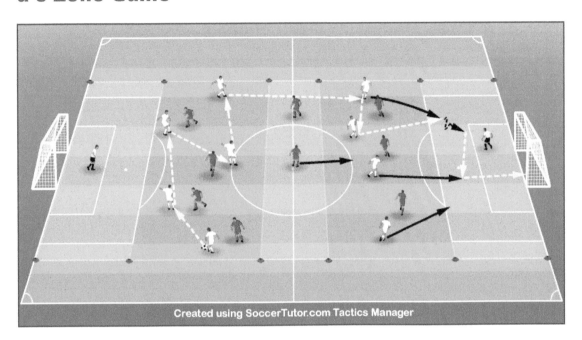

Created using SoccerTutor.com Tactics Manager

Objective

To develop possession in zones and forward passing through the lines.

Description 10 v 10

Using a full pitch, we have 5 different zones with 50 yards width. The zone in the centre of the pitch is 10 yards long.

The white team start the drill as shown, attacking from the back in a 5v4 situation. Their aim is to keep possession under pressure from the 4 defenders and then pass the ball to the opposite zone (the 2 red players in the central zone try to intercept forward passes).

If the ball is played to the other side we have a 4v3+1 (the +1 is a red player who runs across from the central zone). The defenders are not allowed in the end zone until the ball is played in there. If any of the 4 red players win the ball they launch an attack at the opposite end against the 5 white players defending the goal.

If the ball is intercepted in the central zone, the ball is returned to the goalkeeper at the opposite end and the teams change roles with the red team building up play from the back. The 2 middle players move into the red team's low zone and 2 white players from the opposite side move to the middle. The drill starts again with the same objective, but the teams have changed roles. When this happens there will be 5 red vs 4 white in the first zone, the 2 middle players are white and there are 4 red vs 3 white in the other zone (attacking/high zone).

Different rules:

1. In the first zone use limited touches and in the other zone have unlimited touches.
2. In the first zone limit to 3 touches, 2 touches in the other zones and finishing with 1 touch.

GOAL ANALYSIS
Building Up Play from the Back Through the Centre (1)

22-Oct-11

Malaga 0-4 Real Madrid (1st Goal): Higuain - Assist: Di Maria

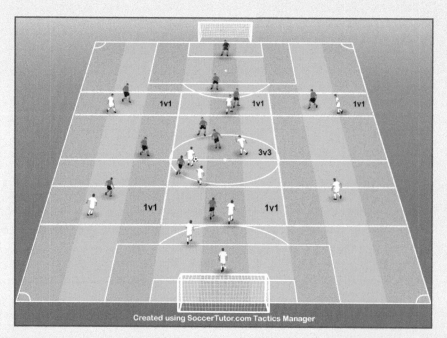

In the first phase of the attack we have different numerical situations in different areas of the pitch which are displayed in the diagram.

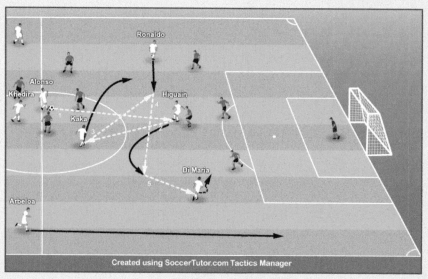

Real move into the second phase of the attack and break through the midfield line of the opposition with good movement and combination play (1 touch football). The ball ends up with Di Maria on the right.

Created using SoccerTutor.com Tactics Manager

Di Maria dribbles inside, Arbeloa makes an outside movement to provide support and create a numerical advantage on the flank (the opposition back 4 are very close together).

Kaka first and then Higuain make diagonal cutting runs in behind the defensive line. Ronaldo moves in the opposite direction to create space. At the correct time, Di Maria plays the ball through to Higuain who dribbles round the goalkeeper and scores.

GOAL ANALYSIS

Building Up Play from the Back Through the Centre (2)

10-Sep-11

Real Madrid 4-2 **Getafe (1ˢᵗ Goal):** Benzema - Assist: Ozil

Ozil has the ball in the low zone. Ronaldo is holding a position inside, so Marcelo moves up on the left side and Carvalho covers his position. We have a 3v3 in the centre, a 2v2 in front of them and a 1v1 in the other areas of the pitch. Ozil dribbles past his opponent, passes to Marcelo and runs forwards, along with Coentrao.

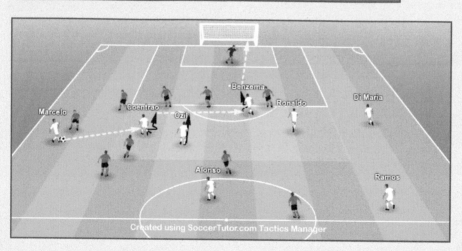

Marcelo passes to Coentrao and now we have a 4v4 situation just in front of the penalty area. Coentrao receives the ball and dribbles up to his direct opponent and then passes inside to Ozil. Ozil passes right again to Benzema who takes a good first touch and scores.

SESSION FOR THIS TOPIC *(2 Practices)*
1. 9v9 (+2) Position Specific 5 Zone Possession Game

Created using SoccerTutor.com Tactics Manager

Objective

To develop possession in zones and exploiting a numerical advantage in the centre.

Description

In an area 30 yards x 25 yards we have 5 zones. In the centre we have 1 large grid which is 15 yards x 15 yards and 2 small zones which are 7.5 yards x 15 yards each. The 2 zones at the sides are both 15 yards x 5 yards. In the big central zone, we have a 3v3 (+2 neutral players) and in the smaller centre zones we have 2v2s. At the sides we have 1v1 situations. Both teams have the same objective which is to maintain possession under pressure.

If a team completes 6 passes or keeps the ball for 8 seconds they get 1 point. If one team passes the ball through all 5 zones without losing possession they get 2 points.

Different rules:

1. Centre backs and wide players limited to 2-3 touches, attackers and inside players unlimited & neutrals have 1 touch.

2. Centre backs, wide players and attackers have unlimited touches, neutral and inside players limited to 1 touch.

Coaching Points

In the Central Zone

1. Within the central zone, the players mainly use passes to feet.

2. Players should check away from their marker before moving to receive (create space).

3. The correct angle, distance and movement is required to provide good support.

4. Good decision making is needed; when to hold the ball, when to play to feet, when to play into space, when to switch the play.

In the Outside Zones

1. Players need to show strength in 1v1 or 2v2 situations.

2. Get your body in between your opponent and the ball (shielding).

3. Communication and coordination needed to time run with pass.

4. Encourage quick one touch combination play.

PROGRESSION

2. Building Up Play from the Back in 1v1 / 2v2 / 3v3 Zones

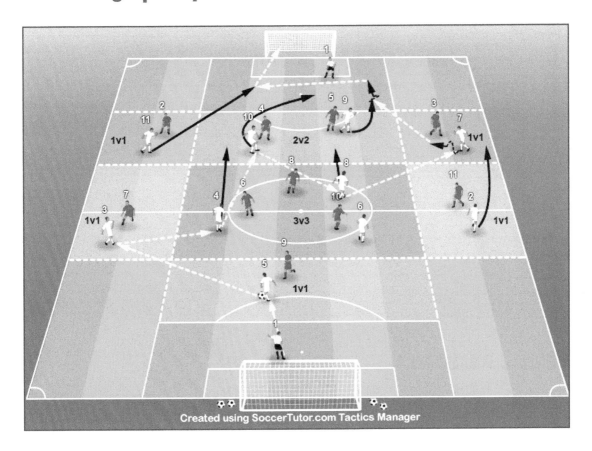

Created using SoccerTutor.com Tactics Manager

Objective

To develop possession in zones and create situations where they have a numerical advantage.

Description

Using a full pitch, we divide the area and players into zones as shown in the diagram.

The drill starts with the white team's goalkeeper. The white team attack from the back and try to create numerical advantages and find solutions against an organised opposition. The white players can change zones but the red players are not allowed. However, if the white team lose possession, the red team are allowed to move freely and attack trying to score on the break.

Coaching Points

1. Use the same points as the previous practice.

2. Forward runs, accuracy, weight of pass and timing of runs in behind are key in this progression.

GOAL ANALYSIS
Build Up Play with a 4v4 Situation on the Flank

10-Sep-11

Real Madrid 4-2 Getafe (4th Goal): Higuain - Assist: Kaka

We have a 4v4 situation at the side and Alonso changes the direction of the play with a pass to Kaka. While the ball is travelling, Higuain makes a cutting run in front of Kaka. Kaka plays a first time pass into his path

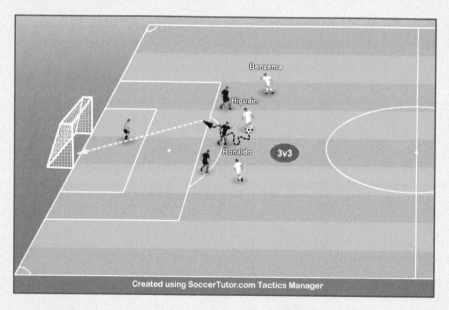

Benzema has also run up and now we have a 3v3 situation just outside the penalty area. Higuain has a 1v1 situation with the central defender and dribbles the ball past him and scores.

PRACTICE FOR THIS TOPIC

1. Building Up Play From the Back with a 4v4 Central Zone

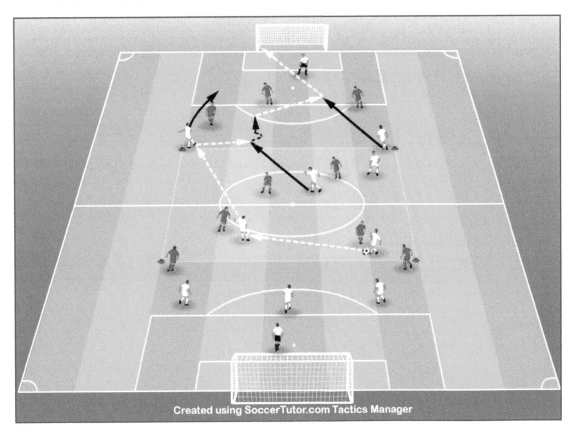

Created using SoccerTutor.com Tactics Manager

Objective

To practice building up play through centre with a typical 4v4 situation.

Description 10 v 10

Using a full pitch we create a zone in the centre of the field (20 yards x 20 yards) and inside it we have a 4v4 situation. At both ends (near the edge of the penalty area) we have 2 attacking players and 3 defenders

One team in the central zone start the drill with the objective to pass to their 2 attacking players outside the zone. One player is allowed to move out of the zone once the pass has been made and we then have a 3v3 situation where the objective is to score past the goalkeeper.

Coaching Points

1. Within the central zone, the 4 attacking players need to show good movement to create space.

2. They should move the ball quickly from the zone to the attacking players.

GOAL ANALYSIS
Creating 1v1 and 2v1 Situations Near the Penalty Area

10-Sep-11
Real Madrid 4-2 Getafe (2nd Goal): Ronaldo

We have a 3v3 situation at the side and Ozil changes the direction of the play, passes to Benzema and then provides quick support for him.

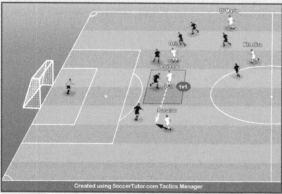

Benzema now has a 1v1 with the centre back, but passes to Ronaldo who is better than him in these situations.

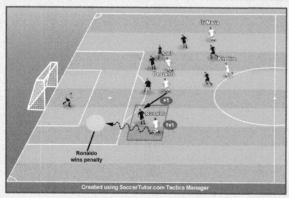

Ronaldo receives the ball and is in a 1v1 situation. Benzema moves to support Ronaldo to create a 2v1 situation and offer the option of a 1-2 combination.

Ronaldo decides to beat his man and is fouled inside the penalty area. He converts the penalty to score.

SESSION FOR THIS TOPIC *(3 Practices)*

1. 'End to End' 3v3 (+3) Possession Game

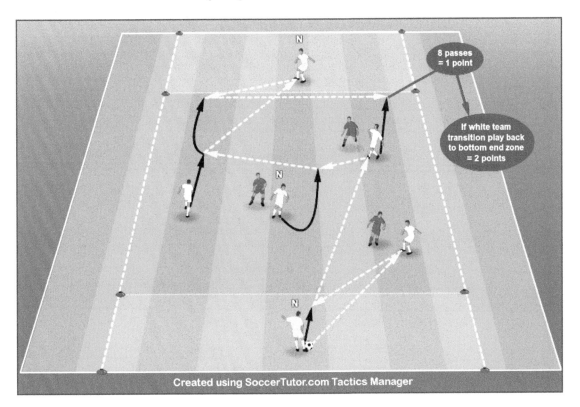

8 passes = 1 point

If white team transition play back to bottom end zone = 2 points

Created using SoccerTutor.com Tactics Manager

Objective

To develop possession, support play, forward passes and exploiting a 1 man advantage in attacking situations.

Description 3 v 3 (+3 Neutral Players)

In an area 12 yards x 12 yards we have a 3v3 (+1 neurtral player) situation and we also we have 1 neutral player at each end in 12 yards x 4 yard zones. The neutral players play with the team in possession and help move the ball from one end zone to the other. If one team completes 8 passes they get 1 point. If they work the ball from one end zone to the other and return it back again they get 2 points.

Different rules:

1. The neutral players have 1 touch and the other players have 2 touches.

2. All players are limited to 1 touch.

Coaching Points

1. Encourage quick, sharp, one touch combination play to move the ball from end to end quickly.

2. The correct angle and distance of support, as well as the quality of the passing is the key here.

PROGRESSION

2. 'End to End' 5v5 (+1) Possession Game

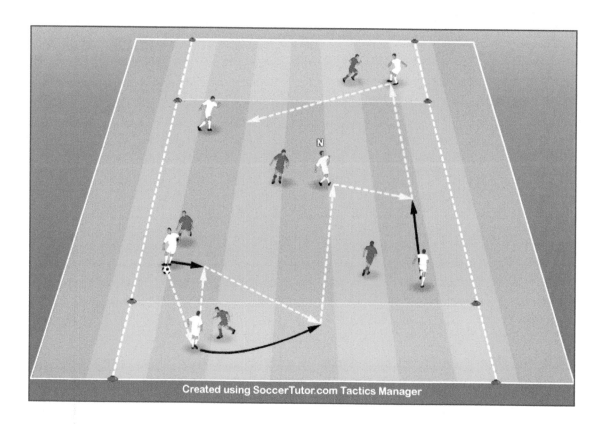

Created using SoccerTutor.com Tactics Manager

Description 5 v 5 (+1 Neutral Player)

In this progression we still have 3v3 (+1 neutral player) in the middle zone, but now we have a 1v1 situation in both of the end zones. The neutral players play with the team in possession and help move the ball from one end zone to the other.

If one team completes 8 passes they get 1 point. If they work the ball from one end zone to the other and return it back again they get 2 points.

Different rules:

1. The neutral players have 2 touches, the inside players have 3 and the outside players have unlimited touches.

2. The neutral players have 1 touch, the inside players have 2 and the outside players have unlimited touches.

PROGRESSION

3. Build Up Through the Centre and Support Play in a 9 Zone Dynamic 10v10 Game

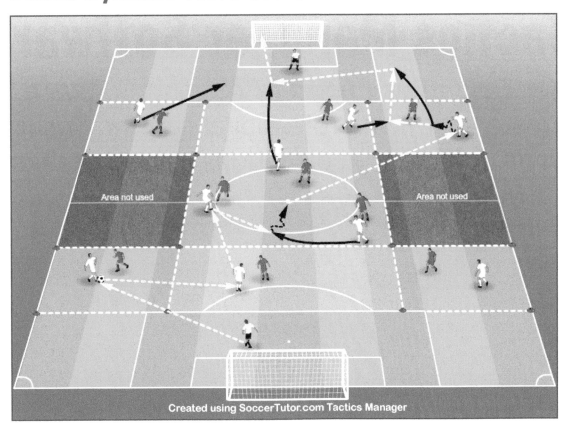

Created using SoccerTutor.com Tactics Manager

Description 10 v 10

Now we use a full pitch and create 7 zones like in the diagram above. In every grid we have an equal number of players for both teams (1v1, 3v3 etc).

In the attacking phase, players can change zones to support each other and create 2v1 numerical advantages. The defending team's players must remain in their respective zones.

The objective is different to the previous examples as both teams look to score. If a defending team wins the ball, they can attack freely and try to score (quick transition for both teams).

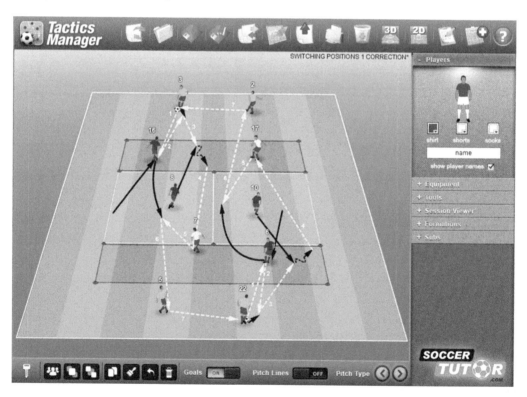

CPSIA information can be obtained
at www.ICGtesting.com
Printed in the USA
BVOW05s1112041117
499011BV00024B/48/P